"In her book, *Marriage Con*
author Cathy Krafve touches

M000296844

lish lasting companionship and influence? This book contains some excellent ideas for helping couples enhance and improve their marriages."

—Josh D. McDowell, speaker and best-selling author
of 151 books including *Evidence that Demands a Verdict*

"Cathy's compassion and care for her readers' marriages is evident from the first page. She pulls back the curtain of her own life and marriage in ways that are vulnerable, humorous, and authentic. Whether you're thinking about getting married or have been married for years you will discover hope and encouragement in this book."

— Ben Sciacca, author of *Meals from Mars:*
A Parable of Prejudice and Providence

"Cathy has put her mark on the real source of power in marriage: intimacy. Under the heading of 'fellowship' she unpacks how a truly powerful marriage, and especially the sexual power in a marriage, isn't illicit power and it isn't even erotic power; it is intimate power. Very few authors are seeing this so clearly. Couples who are friends, who invest in 'fellowship' in life, worship, parenting, fun, affection, 'sparkiness' and in their beds, are the greatest testimony of God's desire for us to have abundant, enriched lives. Cathy reveals the truth of this design in... *Marriage Conversations.*"

— Chris Legg, LPC-S, Pastor of South Spring Baptist Church; Owner
and Lead Therapist at Alethia Family Counseling Center.

"Krafve has crafted a book filled with marital wisdom, advice, and humor that held my interest from the beginning. The honesty in which the author freely shares her own family's triumphs, tragedies, and failures is refreshing. Writing from a wealth of experience, the author demonstrates how small changes improve communication skills in marriage relationships."

— Sandra Merville Hart, author of Civil War romances
including *A Musket in My Hands* and *A Rebel in My House.*

"Reading *Marriage Conversations...* is like sitting beside a sweet sister in Christ while she shares some of the lessons she has learned in her own marriage and in the marriages of others. Cathy's fun personality shines through the pages of the book, and you will walk away encouraged and lifted up."

— LINDSEY BELL, author of *Unbeaten: How Biblical Heroes Rose Above Their Pain (and you can too)* and *Searching for Sanity: 52 Insights from Parents of the Bible*

Marriage
Conversations
from co-existing to cherished

CATHY PRIMER KRAFVE

ST JOSEPH, MISSOURI USA

MARRIAGE CONVERSATIONS: FROM CO-EXISTING TO CHERISED
Copyright © 2021 Cathy Primer Krafve
ISBN: 978-1-936501-56-4

Scripture taken from the New King James Version®. Copyright © 1982 by Thomas Nelson. Used by permission. All rights reserved.

Scripture quotations marked KJV from the King James Version, public domain.

Any webpage addresses or phone numbers used throughout this book are offered as a resource to the reader. These websites are not intended in any way to be or imply an endorsement on the part of CrossRiver Media Group or this book's compilers, nor do we vouch for their content or accuracy for the life of this book.

For more information on Cathy Primer Krafve, please visit — cathykrafve.com

Editor: Debra L. Butterfield
Cover Designer: Carrie Dennis Design

Author is represented by the literary agency of Credo Communications, LLC, Grand Rapids, Michigan, www.credocommunications.net

Printed in the United States of America.

I dedicate this book to the people who inspire me most: my family.

In memory of my parents, Ann and Charlie Primer,
for sharing their stories and loving us
so generously while they were here.

And most of all to David, for stepping into
the adventure of loving each other for a lifetime.

Contents

Introduction

Why This Book?
Because it's so dang practical, real,
and, yes, funny. Plus, it will help.

Imagine evenings in front of a crackling fire after a fun day in the sun. Feel the anticipation of secrets whispered with your best friend and lover. A perfect setting for happily ever after.

As women, many of us go into marriage with stars in our eyes, only to discover marriage is a lot harder than we thought. Bookstore shelves are full of marriage books. Marriage is much more than finding Mr. Right. Some Christian speakers and authors tell us to focus on becoming the right person, as if a human can actually achieve the ideal standard.

Instead, I would propose marriage is the lifelong pursuit of a special kind of intimacy called fellowship. A deeply satisfying marriage requires unity of purpose cultivated over time. Learning to cherish your life-long companion requires a commitment that's sure to be tested. Such oneness may seem out of reach, but it's not impossible to achieve. Intimacy in marriage is an art, not a science.

"Through hell and high water," the old folks used to say, referring to the way their families stuck together during their childhood, enduring the Depression and World War II. When the fifties arrived, my generation's parents pursued educations, found each other, and built their first dream home together. Through the sixties and seventies, they raised families, launching their children into adulthood in the eighties.

Many couples from that amazing generation built marriages that stood the test of decades. How did they do it?

For those who succeeded, their marriages successfully maneuvered through both joys and sorrows for entire lifetimes. Some of us felt defeated almost as soon as we got started. Can we develop the skills to create the marriage conversations we all crave? Yes, we sure can!

I wrote this book for my children, a collection of essays on the essentials of marriage. I have this fear of dropping dead of a heart attack in a parking lot, any parking lot. Okay, I'll admit my parking lot fear is quirky. I'm quirky. I first wrote these ideas to be sure my kids understood the basics. You know, in case of parking lots.

I gave the rough draft to my family for Christmas and held my breath. In my opinion, there's plenty of embarrassing stuff in here. You know, the nitty-gritty stuff you shouldn't mention in public. To complete strangers, for heaven's sake. So why share it at all?

With families in our culture struggling, I wanted my kids to get a head start. We wanted their friends to succeed together and to enjoy authentic conversations. David and I wanted to hold ourselves and our family to a high standard of openness and community.

Marriages are hurting. Our decisions today influence our families for generations after us. Hundreds of years from now, great-grandchildren we will never meet will be carrying around the blessing of the good decisions we make today.

Or, the curse of bad decisions.

Somehow, my family read their rough drafts and skipped over those embarrassing personal parts. They saw beyond to you.

God surrounds us with a legion of amazing women. Yet, as women, we all have moments when we feel alone and isolated. Often comfort and strength can be found in a confession, in a good book, or in a good laugh. Laughter follows the people I love. We all want to share the comfort and strength we've found—and, yes, the laughter as well.

Each chapter examines a specific topic and includes one of our family stories. Or maybe several to let you know we all share in life's joys and sorrows together. Even the quirky parts. At the end of each chapter, I give two personal gifts I hope will help you in your journey. The first gift is a set of personal application questions. The second gift is a prayer I've prayed for myself and my marriage along the way. I hope you'll pray them for yourself and your loved ones. As you pray, allow yourself time to sit quietly before the Lord to hear His answers to your questions.

With these pages, may you discover something new for today. May you know the joy of being cherished in all your relationships, especially your family. My family sends their love and prayers for your ongoing success.

Together, we intend to enjoy a good laugh, too.

Part One
The Whys of Marriage

CHAPTER ONE

Code 44

Why Bother to Marry at All?

*Because marriage is still our best hope for
physical, emotional, and spiritual intimacy.*

T he light switched on, jarring me out of my fitful sleep on the cot next to my dad's bed. The pungent smell of antiseptics jolted my mind into harsh reality.

"Is he breathing? There's no signal on the monitor," demanded the nurse. I cowered in the corner, watching with trepidation as nurses crowded into his room, surrounded his bed, and decided instantly how to proceed.

"Code 44 in Room 5823! Code 44 in Room 5823!"

The automated warning blared throughout the empty hallways of the hospital. A protocol I didn't understand unfolded systematically in front of me. Ignoring me, they focused on his care. They snatched the only chair out of the way to make room for the boxy red defibrillator.

Gently, a nurse ushered me into the hall where the lone chair waited for me, as if I could sit down. Instead, I stood where I could see into the room. From my vantage point I glimpsed Dad's lower left leg and foot. I watched the color leave his skin. Grief squeezed my heart. My lungs froze. I craved Dad's humor in this crisis moment, his natural ability to create fun at the drop of a hat. Memories of campsites, tree forts, fishing, and hammocks dazzled my brain in flashes of heavenly light.

They moved his body to a gurney. Bewildered and frantic, my mind tried to process the scene. What was happening?

"We are moving him to ICU," whispered a nurse coming from his room to stand beside me.

"You mean he's still with us?" I asked, "He's alive?"

My emotions trembled between hope and unreality. Like creeping through fog on a country road in early winter, we were surrounded by light but unable to see the journey ahead of us.

In the days that followed, my dad surprised us all, especially his doctors. While in a medically induced coma, he seemed to respond to Mom's voice with raised eyebrows each time she spoke. Was he working hard to let us know he could hear her?

The doctors constantly reminded us not to get our hopes up. They told us to prepare to end life support. For two weeks, we wondered if it was just our imagination or if he laughed at our jokes. Was he having random spasms or were his shoulders shaking with humor at just the right moment?

Finally, the day came when they took him off his ventilator tube and reduced the sedation. Would he function purposefully? I was the first to arrive when they opened ICU that morning.

"Where's Ann?" he asked when he saw me. The first words out of his mouth were about our sweet mother, who walked in moments behind me with other family members.

The gift of true love. A love that defies reason. A love that defies doctor's orders and human imagination. My dad's love for Mom defied physical boundaries and the laws of the nature, especially human nature. My dad came back for my mom in my favorite love story. In all, they celebrated fifty-eight years of marriage together before Dad left for heaven. They were two of the sweetest lovebirds I know.

I hesitated to share this story of Dad's devotion to our mom because it sounds so storybook perfect. We all want the storybook romance. However, I know the rest of the story. They worked hard to get to the place of true oneness, physically, emotionally, and spiritually.

My dad was known for fun, while my mom got the job done. They came close to throwing in the towel. I saw how their marriage looked in moments of intense distress. Yep, I had a front-row seat. My beautiful mom and dad gave me permission to make a spot for you on the front row. They shared intimate parts of their story here, hoping to encourage others to hang in there.

Doomed or Delighted?

Let's face it, our culture seems pretty hopeless for good marriages. It can feel like the only people with good marriages are the genetic superheroes of the relationship universe. Is a good marriage only for super-gifted people, like only super-smart people make it through medical school or only super-athletes make it to the NBA? If our marriages fall apart, are our kids' marriages doomed? What if we didn't grow up with happily married parents?

I have great news: We all can have hope. Most marriages can improve immediately with a few new skills. Besides, who cares about anyone else's marriage; we just want to be cherished in our own marriage, right? If the big question is why bother to marry at all, the answer is simple. Because marriage remains our best hope for physical, emotional, and spiritual intimacy.

Marriage provides the best path to oneness, that tenderness and intimacy that mark lifelong mutual commitment. Marriage is the place where words like community, intimacy, friendship, oneness, unity can come together if we decide to be intentional in our love for each other.

I watched my parents build tenderness and intimacy into their marriage. Our family suspects Dad's spirit refused to leave Mom. His life on Earth extended beyond all odds, we believe, because the physical, emotional, and spiritual ties between them were so strong. My dad would never have claimed to deserve a dignified death. In fact, he would have scoffed at such a notion.

He spent the last thirty years of his life learning to live as a recovering alcoholic. His humility became a hallmark of his life, but he didn't start out that way. He started out wounded. We all start our marriages with wounds. Can we recover and build redemptive relationships? Yes, the key to a miraculous marriage is fellowship. Fellowship is the gentle art of companionship. However, tenderness is often the missing piece in modern culture.

From Co-existing to Cherished

Nobody wants to merely co-exist in our marriage. We want to feel loved and cherished. Since cherishing each other is an art, let's look at the way artists master their craft.

Even for artists who have a natural aptitude for creating art, mastery requires developing skills. The artist must devote herself to sketching, for instance. She must collect tools, such as pencils, charcoal, paint, and easels. Noting the lighting, she must study the perspective lines of a scene, the interplay of color, and the emotional mood of a subject. Finally, with care and devotion, a process develops, eventually resulting in mastery.

Exactly like artists practice to eventually create art masterpieces, we begin by studying and practicing skills to create great conversations in marriage, as in all our relationships. We can learn a lot from Jesus, the master communicator. One thing about Jesus—He understands our needs. He cares about the things you and I care about. He doesn't bore us with long dissertations when it comes to defining marriage. He gets right to the point: oneness. Leave it to Jesus to share a profound truth that changes everything! As we study Him, we equip ourselves to be masters in gentle judicious lifestyles leading to cherished relationships.

With gratitude, I share a small part of my parents' grand story to say there is hope for the rest of us. Imperfect people create healthy marriages all the time. If Ann and Charlie can do it, so can we. While marriage can be challenging, even heartbreaking at times, creating intimacy is extravagantly joyful.

Dad lived for a year and a half after that Code 44 moment. We all said our goodbyes to him in a clean, quiet room at hospice. In that bonus time, we got a final glimpse of the truly loving, wise, thoughtful, funny, creative person God designed Dad to be all along. In his weakest moments physically, his brightest attributes glowed. The poignant tenderness between my parents was palpable, each moment a measured treasure. The weather was chilly and peaceful on a fall evening when Mom held Dad as she said her tender good-bye. He comforted her, then a few hours later he slipped away to heaven. We're pretty sure we know exactly who Dad hangs out with up there. He always sought out our favorite fun people. We think Dad is teaching the young people to jitterbug while he watches for his all-time favorite partner to join him.

We All Crave Companionship

God designed us each one for an emotionally intimate, loving relationship with Him. No wonder we all crave companionship. We all want to be loved. Everyone does. We're designed by God to seek a relationship with Him. However, throughout our modern culture, people looking for love often fail to find it.

When it comes to relationships, there's great news, though. God loves second chances. He can forgive any sin and heal any past or present wounds. Astonishingly, God loves second chances so much He sent His Son to pay for them. Jesus' death on the cross paid for you and for any hurt you carry. Like my dad chose my mom and came back for her, Jesus chose you and rose from the dead to prove His ability to love you faithfully.

May I suggest you make a decision today that can change all your relationships forever? God sent His Son, Jesus, to seek you out. Jesus is the One who is lovingly referred to as the Bridegroom.[1] He demonstrated that miracles, joy, life, sacrifice, and resurrection are simply who He is. I invite you, if you don't know Him, to begin an intimate, loving relationship with Him today. As you begin to trust Him, you will marvel at how He will help you build fellowship in all your relationships. Have no fear, Jesus loves you with unfailing, tender love.

No matter what else people say about Jesus, everyone seems to agree Jesus was an amazing teacher when He walked the earth. I love the way He took the hardest questions and boiled down truth so we can all

---

1   See Matthew 9:14–15; Mark 2:18–20; Luke 5:33–35; John 3:29.

benefit. He shared many amazing truths about marriage. Keep reading as we examine them together.

In Case You Were Wondering...

We all have questions. Jesus was not afraid of questions. They don't have to be scary for us either. I pulled some of my favorites from our Camp Krafve, CathyKrafve.com, website for this book.

If my marriage is terrible, am I doomed? Absolutely not. You are not doomed, but you may need courage and some new skills.

Clearly, humans are natural romantics who somehow, against all odds, keep believing in the ideal of true love. Two marriages and two divorces later, we still show up at our friends' third try. Naively perhaps, we want to believe this time the marriage will be happy and will last. Human nature must carry a common, effervescent hope making us want to be married, even when we know it can hurt.

Instinctively, we seem to know there must be a way to create fulfilling marriages. We may even notice people who seem to have done it. Effective communication skills for marriage can be taught and learned. I watched my parents negotiate the heck out of marriage. It took work and courage, but you already know the end of their story. Their work paid off in huge dividends.

Since we're designed for a loving relationship with God, it follows that humans naturally crave those kinds of relationships with other people. In fact, we love because God loved us first.

"We love Him because He first loved us" (1 John 4:19). Deep satisfaction flows out of the thought that God loved us first. The idea of His initiating love affirms our value. We can free ourselves to love from whole hearts, as we ponder God's love for us.

Small decisions become the daily mini-miracles we anticipate with joyful expectancy. We must ponder the kind of relationships we want if we want whole hearts, not broken ones.

You can formulate strategies so fabulous and personal you won't even need anyone else's participation to get started. We don't have to be sneaky, victimized, or wounded. Like my beautiful mom, we can simply live a miraculous life, firmly and patiently loving all those around us.

As you read, may I recommend you record your personal revelations in a private place like a journal? Later, you will recognize your growth and be encouraged. I hope you laugh. You may cry. You will discover some new strategies to improve the group dynamics in your home, at work, at church, and, well, just about anywhere. Best of all, you will know you are not alone in your struggles or your triumphs. Oh, what joy!

Pause, Ponder, Pray, Then Proceed

1. Understanding your needs: To what lengths are you willing to go to create new dynamics in your relationships, especially your marriage? This is an important question to answer for yourself.

What prayer requests about marriage are so crucial and specific that you will write them down so you know when they are answered?

2. Identifying your worth: As women, we often fail to appreciate our own worth. It's a common problem. Create an ad as a mail-order bride and sell your strengths to a pretend potential husband. What did you write about your own value? Give yourself freedom to be totally silly and braggadocious. Laugh, but know what is true. You are valuable in innumerable ways.

3. Envisioning your future: If God offered you anything, what would you ask Him to do for you, His beloved daughter, the apple of His eye? Please turn to Him in prayer and ask for that very thing now.

Write a personal definition of a good marriage. What would a marriage look like that you deem worthy of your heart-felt commitment? Now share that description with a trustworthy friend. When we share our most personal dreams and fears with trustworthy friends, we unlock the door to wholeheartedness in all our relationships.

My prayer for you, with my love

Dear God, You are a companion to us in ways we cannot comprehend. We easily feel abandoned, unwanted, and alone. Please bless my sister with a new and deeper knowledge of who You truly are. Help her shed any wounded thoughts keeping her from knowing You. You love her beyond her comprehension. Bless her with a vivid awareness of Your tenderness for her. Help her heart be whole, not broken. Allow Your love for her to energize her and inspire her with hope and joy.

From Psalm 3, we offer You this praise: "But You, O LORD, *are* a shield for me, My glory and the One who lifts up my head" (Psalm 3:3).

To pray for yourself

Beloved good Father, You are the Designer of marriage. Thank You for Your Son who expressed Your love for me in sacrifice because He values me as worthy. Help me shake off any feelings of unworthiness and rejection as I sit in Your presence. Let me get to know You in new ways today.

What do You want to teach me so I can bring home fellowship in all my relationships? Help me trust You as together we develop a beautiful future for me. Give me courage to be vulnerable and reveal this beautiful heart You gave me. Bless me now because that's Your heart's desire. In Jesus' name I pray. Amen.

"I'm convinced that there's a song, a dance, and a path to laughter for every human emotion." — **Brene Brown**, *The Gifts of Imperfection*

CHAPTER TWO

Catching Mom

Why is sex crucial to the way marriage is supposed to work?

Because Jesus clearly taught that sexual intercourse is the initiating act of marriage.

Dad chased my mom until she let him catch her. He always told the story the same way. Dad acknowledged, with a twinkle in his eye, the victory he felt at capturing the heart of such a smart and talented gal. As a child, I believed my dad literally ran after Mom in the streets of Austin, Texas. I pictured him in preppy clothes, pursuing my mom dressed in a 1950s poodle skirt and pink cashmere sweater set. In my imagination, they're running to my grandparents' house on Rio Grande Street.

My other mental image of my parents' courtship happens on a bright green tennis court a few blocks from campus. She trounced him, a poor medical student with virtually no athletic ability by Dad's own account. If you didn't believe how un-athletic he was, he would remind you he claimed membership on the Austin High School football team only because they counted water boys as part of the team. Dad liked to say he almost didn't marry Mom because she beat him at tennis.

Later, when I was a student at the university, I spent an afternoon circling the blocks near campus looking for tennis courts. The courts of my imagination were created by one of the most vivid storytellers I've ever known—my dad.

One thing I'm not imagining is the power of the chemistry between my parents. God dished up a lot of chemistry when He created the universe, and Mom and Dad got a heaping helping of it. Dad always said he almost missed out on medical school because of chemistry, but when it came to romancing Mom, he mastered it.

They settled into a rhythm of Mom raising kids and Dad going to work every day. One day, I surprised them as I charged in from playing outside. I suddenly realized I was not alone as I sped through a dim family room. From a shadowy corner of the room, Mom's whispery giggle gave them away. My mom curled up in my dad's lap in a big easy chair. Even as a kid, I realized there was something special about the way they whispered together when no one else was around.

If only we could all enjoy that kind of romantically charged chemistry. My folks practiced the art of flirting with each other all their lives. They returned to the fellowship and commitment they built together despite tense times in their marriage. Ongoing romantic chemistry marked their love for each other. Sometimes in our marriages we think the embers are dead, hope burnt up. However, romance, sex, and the physical side of our marriages are crucial parts of marriage. There is power in attraction. Therefore, romance requires our attention and nurture.

I watched for a lifetime as my parents' relationship evolved, and yet they always devoted themselves to keeping things sparky at each stage of life. Charlie and Ann managed to hang in there, in spite of the way alcoholism and previous trauma affected their relationship. Just as they flirted and cherished each other to the end, so can we. Warm affection built over a lifetime marked their relationship all along the way.

When we fall in love, we don't necessarily realize we're committing to a lifelong process of healing together. Single-hearted devotion exemplifies the idea of the two becoming one. Amazingly, my parents overcame all obstacles to demonstrate true intimacy, the unity of spirit, soul, and body. But there's so much confusion about how to define marriage, it's a good idea to really examine which definition we think is true.

The Common Definition of Marriage

Today, in modern culture, marriage is commonly defined as a long-term, unique commitment of two people to love each other, warts and all. The relationship is acknowledged to have a sexual component. The commitment is not necessarily lifelong, and it may not be encumbered by legalities, like getting a license at the courthouse. Many people even resist the label marriage for their most intimate relationship.

When we think of intimacy, we often think first of sex, not spiritual or emotional oneness, and certainly not fellowship. We know sex in marriage matters. Yet, the words *fellowship* and *chemistry* are thrown around so much they lose their zip. Still, fellowship and chemistry are inseparable links in good marriages. When sex is great, all is right with the world, but sex can also be emotionally disturbing.

Fortunately, God is on our side in this essential arena of sparking up the chemistry in marriage. How great is that? Therefore, let's lay a groundwork of simple, foundational truths so we can be armed for success. We'll start with how God defines marriage.

"How does God define marriage?" Joanne, a gifted Bible translator and linguist, asked me one day as we walked around the block. Imagine my befuddlement.

"Isn't it somewhere in the Old Testament?" I asked, even though I couldn't think of any place. "Leviticus maybe?" (I figure if I don't remember it, it's probably in Leviticus.)

"Cathy, think about it. What did Jesus say about marriage?" Joanne asked again.

"The two shall become one?" I guessed. Bingo! At that moment it was the only thing I knew for sure Jesus actually said about marriage.

As I walked the block with my friend that day, I knew I needed to rethink how I perceived sex. Aren't oneness and sex in marriage tied together somehow? I knew I needed to give oneness more thought. Could Jesus be saying marriage begins with sexual intercourse? If marriage begins with sexual intercourse, what other truths had I missed?

As I pondered and searched the Scriptures, I soon discovered God designed sexual intimacy to initiate emotional and spiritual intimacy as well. We are designed to enjoy fellowship for a lifetime. Physical oneness illustrates the ultimate oneness available in marriage. Yet, there's more to the story as I quickly recognized, studying the way others received Jesus' ideas.

Jesus, the master communicator, always shared profound truth, changing lives all around him. He demonstrated the most authentic love. Only God's heart could conceive of a sacrificial love willing to die on the cross to restore our lives from the rot of sin and selfishness. His design for marriage invites us to understand love in a whole new way. We're invited to communicate our way to tender companionship with Him and each other.

The Traditional Christian Definition

Most Christians are quick to define marriage as the union of one man to one woman for a lifetime, an exclusive commitment, affirmed in a church ritual and legally binding. Christians often include the word *covenant*, meaning God is in the process and both parties commit to loving each other unconditionally without regard to what they will receive in return. The common expectation is that you commit to each other, regardless of the circumstances.

To understand how Jesus' own definition of marriage challenged the scholars of His day, we may want to take a close look at their reaction to His ideas. Legal experts challenged Him with a tough question about divorce on this controversial topic of marriage: "The Pharisees also came to Him, testing Him, and saying to Him, 'Is it lawful for a man to divorce his wife for *just* any reason?'" (Matthew 19:3). They are asking the same question we still ask today: When is divorce okay?

The Pharisees were the religious experts, the smart people of the day, the guys with the equivalent of PhDs from Harvard and Yale. Cultural celebrities, they had dibs on making and keeping the rules about the temple sacrifices. The real money and power poured out of the temple sacrifices, a booming economic business. A word from the Pharisees incited riots, for instance, if temple rituals didn't conform to their expectations.[2]

I imagine the scholars thought they had Jesus stumped. They usually gave the tests.[3] Who had the nerve to give them a test? However, Jesus handled their questions with perceptive understanding, just as He can handle our toughest questions. I love the way Jesus understood these Pharisees.

Jesus' purposeful answers refuted the Pharisees' false understanding. He offered them wisdom for their own marriages because He deeply loved these confused men.

Naturally, they demanded sections of trusted Scripture to verify His premise. He chose Genesis, the first book of the Torah, the most beloved of Jewish teachings. Torah means "instruction and offers a way of life for those who follow it."[4]

From the beginning, the Torah confirmed the centrality of the one flesh relationship to marriage. Genesis teaches: "'This *is* now bone of my bones, And flesh of my flesh; She shall be called Woman, Because she was taken out of Man.' Therefore a man shall leave his father and mother and be joined to his wife, and they shall become one flesh" (Genesis 2:23–24).

Our culture trivializes sex. Hollywood deceives us daily with ridiculous scenarios about sex. Is it any wonder discouragement overwhelms us when the chemistry in marriage seems to go out?

But sex is key to marriage according to Jesus. This is great news! Why? Because Jesus cuts through all the noise about relationships and sex. He understands our confusion and gives us clarity.

Jesus' Definition of Marriage

Jesus clarified marriage is initiated by sexual intercourse. The two shall become one. God designed sex with the purpose of bringing two people together in order to initiate a lifelong relationship. Marriage's

2   Bruce Chilton, *Rabbi Jesus: An Intimate Biography,* (New York Image Books, Doubleday, 2000), 121–123, 219–221.

3   James 1:2–15, *The New Greek English Interlinear New Testament,* Translators: Robert Brown et al, Editors: Kurt Aland et al. (Wheaton, Illinois: Tyndale House Publishers, 1990), United Bible Society.

4   Torah, https://en.wikipedia.org/wiki/Torah, accessed 09-17-16

goal is to know intimate fellowship and unfailing commitment. This process, in turn, draws us close in intimate fellowship with the One who designed marriage. Others are drawn to Him, as a result.

Jesus taught an amazing foundational principle about oneness. Knowing sexual intercourse is the initiating act of marriage gives us the courage and the stamina to keep pursuing true marital oneness, and yes, even chemistry. God designed us to experience growing, tender chemistry in our marriages as our lives progress. But we should define chemistry the way God does and not the way Hollywood does. To understand the overarching purpose of God's design of marriage, unity crowned by fellowship, we must understand God's purpose in sexual intercourse.

"And He [Jesus] answered and said to them [the Pharisees], 'Have you not read that He who made *them* at the beginning 'made them male and female,' and said, 'For this reason a man shall leave his father and mother and be joined to his wife, and the two shall become *one flesh*'? So then, they are *no longer two but one flesh*. Therefore what God has joined together, let not man separate'" (Matthew 19:4–6, emphasis mine).

Jesus' teaching was so radical even His disciples shook their heads in astonishment. They were hanging out with a relationship genius who tried His best to teach them all the good stuff. Yet still His best friends responded to Him, "If such is the case of the man with *his* wife, it is better not to marry" (Matthew 19:10).

Probably we've all asked the same question—Why bother to get married at all? As women, we live in a terrific time to be single because we have more opportunities than any other time in history. Many single women today say they would rather be single than married to the wrong guy. I wholeheartedly endorse the resolve to forego marriage, rather than feel trapped in a hostile situation at home. We must choose wisely when marrying. We all gain clarity about our own personal decisions for our future when we understand God's intention behind marriage.

Jesus handled His disciples' bewilderment with calm reassuring consolation. He knew He taught unexpected truth. To modern ears, his response may seem really strange.

"But He said to them, 'All cannot accept this saying, but only *those* to whom it has been given: For there are eunuchs who were born thus from *their* mother's womb, and there are eunuchs who were made eunuchs by men, and there are eunuchs who have made themselves eunuchs for the kingdom of heaven's sake. He who is able to accept it, let him accept *it*'" (Matthew 19:11–12).

Say what? Let's start with a very unfamiliar word for modern folks—*eunuchs*. Eunuchs were men who did not have sexual relations. Some were eunuchs by choice, some due to a tradition of making slaves unable to consummate a physical relationship. By addressing this subject boldly, Jesus clarified an important fact—people rarely forego sex. Simultaneously, He acknowledged sex as a significant part of life.

I like the way Jesus jumped right over the Pharisees' original question; they basically asked, "Is it okay to get divorced?" Ironically, the Pharisees thought they knew the answer. They believed marriage was a religious ritual, sanctioned by some sort of societal legal mechanism. Thus, they implied it could be dissolved with another legal action, putting the legal authorities at odds with the religious ones.

Essentially, they thought their little test would create a gotcha moment for Jesus. They wanted to know who was in charge. The religious leaders or the government?

Instead, Jesus answered the better question, the question they did not ask. How does God define marriage? If they did not understand how God defines marriage, they could not possibly understand divorce. Jesus simply redirected their focus from divorce to the fundamental truth of oneness in marriage. He emphasized divorce results from hardheartedness, as it still does today in so many modern marriages.

Jesus Loved the Pharisees

Jesus gently but firmly handled their question without rudeness because He loved the Pharisees. Often, we forget Jesus loved all people, even annoying ones. He knew better understanding would serve the best interests of these beloved scholars. He cared about their marriages, too. He answered with their best interests in mind. His answer is in our best interests as well.

We're often taught to read Matthew 19 and think, Okay, got it. God has a plan for my marriage, so I better make it work. "So then, they are no longer two but one flesh. Therefore what God has joined together, let not man separate" (Matthew 19:6). If we tell the truth, we may think divorce is not an option, so I am totally trapped in this lifeless marriage. Jesus taught something radically different from what we traditionally have been led to believe. Perhaps now is a terrific time to push pause and think about marriage a different way. A fresh look shows Jesus resurrecting a clear idea. God wanted a personal relationship with us from the beginning, like Adam's relationship with God in the garden (Genesis 3:8–10).

Remember the leaders of Jesus' day promoted strict rules associated with religion. Jesus gave God credit for the one flesh union, without the trappings of a ceremony or the blessing of religious leaders. He reclaimed marriage as God's domain. Jesus spoke a plain and simple idea, unencumbered by man-made religious trappings. A man and a woman make the decision to marry, clearly delineated by sexual intercourse. God established the plan for marriage, not religious or legal scholars.

Better yet, Jesus wanted to demonstrate on Earth what fellowship and oneness can look like in a relationship with Him. Since God designed humans for companionship with Him, no wonder we all crave oneness. Knowing humankind's propensity for selfishness, God created chemistry in the mix to draw people together. People can be drawn together as surely as God created protons and electrons to naturally seek each other.

God always keeps our best interests at heart. Sexual drive gives way to tender affection over the years. As we age, a devoted union develops into a beautiful picture of the trusting, comfortable relationship God wants to have with each of us. Marriage is not the only way to develop oneness with God. But if we choose marriage, the purpose of our marriage is to reflect intimacy with Him.

Jesus clearly taught sexual intercourse as the initiating act of marriage. God designed sexual intercourse to join a woman physically together with her husband, according to Jesus. By saying it this way, Jesus taught an important truth. God thinks our sex life is important, just like we do. The Creator has an opinion about our best welfare, even our sexual well-being. What a refreshing and strengthening truth!

Sexual intercourse begins marriage, but it's not the end-all. Many couples in lifeless marriages continue to have sex without cultivating fellowship at deeper spiritual and emotional levels. Oneness results from cherishing each other unconditionally and tenderly with devotion. Physical, sexual intimacy is only the initial picture of fellowship in all other areas of marriage.

God intends to use our marriages to bless others as we develop fellowship with our spouse. Other people are naturally drawn to the love we share. When others recognize God's blessings in our lives and marriages, they may become interested in seeking Him as the source of all true fellowship and intimacy. Additionally, our children learn to trust the fellowship we offer as they witness our persevering love for each other.

Key Ingredients to an Excellent Definition

What does a great marriage look like to you? Please consider the following ideas because these seem to be consistent with what Jesus taught.

- Marriage begins with sexual intercourse.
- Marriage joins two people together, spiritually, emotionally, and physically.
- Marriage draws us into intimate, lifelong commitment and tenderness with each other.
- Marriage reflects the infinite fellowship and unfailing love offered by God, the One who designed marriage.
- Marriage purposely draws others into fellowship with Him.

To create tender marriage conversations, couples must pursue healthy habits, honoring each other. My parents kept things sparky and full of chemistry for a lifetime. Intentionally cherishing each other takes guts and perseverance. In the end, the way they cherished each other daily created a fellowship that was breathtaking for those of us who observed the process over a lifetime.

"We want a marriage like theirs," David and I agreed as we left my dad's funeral.

But even with more than thirty years of marriage at that moment, we knew it would require hard work and some serious rebooting. For all of us, strategically enhancing fellowship in our relationships can start today.

In Case You Were Wondering...

Perhaps our hearts treasure the wisdom Jesus taught because He seeks us out for spiritual oneness with Him. We crave fellowship because our design demands it.

What about a husband who seems impatient and demanding about sex? Men and women do have different needs when it comes to sex. It's only fair to grant our husbands some grace if we in turn expect them to meet some of our needs. Some needs can only be met by a spouse.

Clearly, finding healthy parameters and expectations is crucial. If it seems complicated, we can relax. Just about the time you think you have it all figured out, pregnancies, health issues, or age complicate your relationship yet again. Learning to communicate clearly about your insecurities, needs, and pleasures will take many conversations over a lifetime.

Each stage of life presents its own challenges from a practical point of view. Certainly, I'm not a counselor. I hope you seek out professional help from trusted advisors. All along life's path, couples must renegotiate and communicate as sexual needs change. Patience and insight become our best allies in cherishing a lover for a lifetime.

We all feel overwhelmed sometimes. In fact, I experience my loneliest moments when my husband and I are "out of fellowship." Our hurt feelings often override our sense of joint purpose and appreciation for each other. In those recurring moments, we find sparky chemistry challenging.

Gratefulness lights the spark of fellowship. I make a habit of writing down why I married my husband anytime I get mad at him. Usually, I immediately feel slightly more grateful, no matter how angry or hurt I feel.

You can rejoice because God wants to do wondrous things in your own heart and life. That alone is a reason to be thankful, even if the hubby (or ex-husband) still behaves badly. We can find reason to be thankful in the gentleness of a breeze, the pleasure of a good book, or the loyalty of a wise friend, as we keep safe and secure.

Please keep reading. This is only the beginning of many conversations about marriage. Other women ask these same tough questions. By asking hard questions, we will find answers. Together, we will explore a bunch of ideas to help you have the conversations you're craving in your marriage now, even if your husband takes forever to catch on.

Pause, Ponder, Pray, Then Proceed

As we reflect on Jesus' teaching on marriage, His ideas run through our souls like the whisper of the wind. For those with hearts able to hear, there is a beautiful secret. The truth—marriage begins with sexual intercourse—whispers understanding to our soul.

1. Understanding your needs: Since Jesus taught that sexual intercourse is the initiating act of marriage, experiences in your past may complicate your ability to be healthy now. Which clergy, counselor, or trustworthy friend can listen as you process your past and move into your future? Please make an appointment this week to get some healthy feedback.

2. Identifying your worth: List three ways you're encouraged by knowing God has a personal interest in your marriage and its chemistry. When you describe your heart's most attractive quality, what do you say? It's so important to know you are naturally attractive because God designed you.

3. Envisioning your future: How will companionship look in your life, starting first thing in the morning when you wake up? Start a list now of past, present, and future things that make you happy about your husband. Begin a prayer habit today, starting with thanking God for those things you cherish in your husband.

If you've been wounded by marriage, ask God to heal any fresh pain surfacing as a result of reading this book. He offers new comfort each morning for our heart's broken places, dear one.

My prayer for you, with my love

Dear God, marriage (and life in general) can feel very lonely. May my beautiful sister experience Your care for her spiritual, emotional, and physical well-being. Please let her rest in complete fellowship with You, the One who created the universe. Allow her the time and energy to tenderly care for herself as a way of expressing her respect for You. Please give her understanding of the powerful life designed for her by You, the universe's great Chemist.

We turn to You together, agreeing with the psalmist, "Hear me when I call, O God of my righteousness! You have relieved me in *my* distress; Have mercy on me, and hear my prayer" (Psalm 4:1).

To pray for yourself

Good Father, You are the One who designed me for fellowship with You. Please teach me how my life can reflect Your tender companionship. Give me power and strength in my present circumstances, please, O Lord. Teach me to live the words Jesus spoke. When I feel lonely, remind me that You stand ready to embrace me in Your love. You cherish me and teach me my worth. When I feel unworthy, help my attention focus on You, the One who loves me unconditionally and sacrificially. Give me poise in my frustration. As I live joyfully and purposefully today, give me strength and courage about my marriage. Intervene on my behalf because I belong to You. May I enjoy Your favor today. Bless me now because that's Your heart's desire. In Jesus' name I pray. Amen.

"Jesus wants us to come. He's sending His servants out to tell the people standing at the fences and in the libraries that they're invited to the party. He's sending you an invitation too, in the sunrise, in the sound of a bird, or in the smell of coffee drifting from the kitchen. The one who has invited you is way more powerful than any of the impediments we think we're facing and He has just one message for us. He leans forward and whispers quietly to each of us, 'There's more room.'" — **Bob Goff**, *Love Does*

CHAPTER THREE

Mom's Parents Were Sparky

Why is fellowship the best foreplay?
Because fellowship answers the
universal craving for oneness.

My grandparents, Mom's parents, were sparky. They flat out flirted with each other. You couldn't miss the electricity in the air. Other nuances intrigued me as a little girl. My grandmother, Meme, had lacy negligees hanging on her hook in the bathroom. Her nighttime attire looked like something out of a 1940s Hollywood movie wardrobe. When I was a kid, I thought she was way too old for such things, but she was around fifty, much younger than I am now.

She expressed her affection for Granddaddy in the way she obsessively swept the floor. She cleared a path for him because he was nearly blind with cataracts. She kept his bananas and cheese puffs off-limits to us kids. A stack of clean, ironed handkerchiefs graced his drawer because he believed a gentleman always carried a hankie.

No one else would label these gestures as romantic, certainly not foreplay. Yet, those small habits and a zillion others expressed abundant affection. Small gestures of affection were the foundation of their mutual understanding and spark. My grandparents spoke volumes of tenderness in words of affirmation, acts of service, gifts, quality time, and physical touch long before love languages became ingrained in our thinking.[5]

---

5   Gary Chapman, *The 5 Love Languages: The Secret to Love that Lasts,* (Chicago: Northfield Publishing, 1992).

We all want a marriage that becomes a sanctuary for ourselves and others. We hope someday our grandchildren will say they saw a lifetime of love by hanging out with us. We may not always know what fellowship in marriage looks like, yet instinctively we know it's bound to translate into a fun, sparky relationship and great sex.

Both my grandparents worked hard to provide a comfortable upbringing for their kids. On Saturdays, simply because he liked to hang out with her, Granddaddy let Meme drive him all over town hunting for garage sales to stretch the family budget. He found her energy entertaining. He smiled constantly at her, the twinkle in his eyes magnified by his coke-bottle glasses.

The Next Generation Comes Together

Imagine how invigorating that atmosphere was for my dad after growing up in a formal home. Even as a kid, I thought it was odd that Dad's parents slept in separate bedrooms. I understand now their relationship was complicated and formal because my grandfather wanted to treat my grandmother tenderly due to some health issues. They were married for almost fifty years when she died.

In contrast, Dad's family heritage captivated my mom. I'm sure the formality of their family traditions contributed to the attraction my mom felt for Dad. She was the first in her immediate family to go to college. Dad's world seemed sophisticated and polished to my mom. The formality practiced by my dad's parents must have intrigued her.

Meme was an avid Red Cross volunteer, channeling her natural energy during and after WWII into volunteering. Observing Dad's family, Mom quickly noted how to extend her education with community service.

My dad witnessed community service from the vantage point of watching his dad serve a lifetime in public health. He grew up in a home devoted to serving others through education, reflected in an immense library of leather-bound books in multiple languages. The smell of pipe tobacco still conjures memories of quiet afternoons spent in the library first collected by my dad's grandfather.

My dad brought to their marriage the tenderness and loyalty he had seen his father exemplify. My mom brought an expectation they would be partners in life and have fun in the process. Their two backgrounds combusted to create terrific romantic energy. Thus, they started their marital adventure happy, but clueless about the daily hurdles they would face together. Growing up, I watched them struggle to meld their ideas, expectations, and baggage into a marriage designed to last a lifetime.

We think we're all grown up when we walk down the aisle. In reality, we are just getting started. Coming together, not only do we interweave our weaknesses and strengths, we also navigate both sets of family values and histories. Plus, there's all the stuff we didn't get growing up, including some stuff we don't yet know we are missing. All those factors get magnified by any change to the relationship, even normal changes like adding babies to the family.

Foreplay, Sparkiness, and Fellowship

Since Jesus acknowledged sexual intercourse as a defining part of marriage, we feel free to talk about how sexy dynamics can spark up our marriage. The fellowship Mom and Dad developed in the process of unifying their divergent backgrounds and baggage created a palpable kind of chemistry. Even as a kid, I knew their sparkiness was a direct result of the fellowship, fun, and common purpose they created together. I didn't hear the term foreplay until I was an adult, but now I know fellowship is the best foreplay.

Can we trust Hollywood's definition of foreplay? Of course not. Foreplay begins with a simple gesture—a look or a touch. The relationship blossoms, and foreplay takes on more urgency. When we date, foreplay is a natural reflection of our enjoyment of each other, a step toward joining together in sexual intercourse if the relationship progresses.

Once we marry, sexual intercourse becomes an expected part of the relationship. Those tender exchanges of foreplay leading up to sex can easily get crowded out of our busy lives.

To reclaim the joy of foreplay, we better define it clearly. Men and women often view foreplay differently, since we're wired so differently. Whole books are written about what best expresses caring. We should study our own happiness triggers. Knowledge of what communicates positive vibes to your spouse is a treasure to seek!

Perhaps a wink or a kiss or a caress, or, heck, that certain dress triggers your husband's libido. No matter the various ways sexual interest is conveyed, the spoken and unspoken signals reflect tender vulnerability.

For both spouses, long before anything else happens, the stage is set by a sense of safety and belonging. Foreplay constitutes oh-so-much much more than a wink and a kiss!

The Foreplay of Great Fellowship

No better word for those feelings of safety and belonging exists than fellowship. We think of fellowship as something for church groups only. But a healthy marriage is the natural habitat of fellowship. In fact, fellowship for the whole family flows out of the fellowship created by the parents.

Obviously, fellowship in marriage encompasses so much more than foreplay. Living together as tender companions for a lifetime necessitates fostering acceptance, not rejection. For couples who master healthy conversation, the fellowship they share together naturally produces the kind of sparky intimacy we might call foreplay.

In contrast, rejection in any form quickly destroys a romantic moment and corrodes trust. Therefore, fellowship grows strong in an environment of mutual respect and acceptance. Seriously, don't we all want a marriage hot with passion and warm with affection. We certainly do not want one hot with anger and rejection.

When we trust God, the great Chemist, with the process of marriage, we are melding two valuable metals, copper and zinc, into an even stronger metal, bronze. Just as alloying copper and zinc together creates the inseparable union of bronze, so a good marriage melds two different people together into one. Heat inevitably binds or spoils the process. As heat binds metal into a stronger union, so the challenges of life can bind two people together for a lifetime.

Somehow, we instinctively know the sexual part of marriage is essential to creating a happy home. Especially after a good night's rest, flirting and playing may seem likely, a happy fantasy within reach. Sadly, our daydreams don't always hold up to reality. Managing all the moving parts of real life often crowds out intimacy.

It's easy to give up on having great sex, especially the foreplay component. Rushing through sex, as tempting and crazy as it seems in movies, seriously threatens marriage, especially when rushing becomes the habit. Unity takes time and attention. Nurturing conversations build trust. So, one reason fellowship creates the best foreplay is because savoring time together communicates devotion.

A couple who savors time together naturally draws together, even physically. Fellowship is the best foreplay because it answers our universal craving for oneness, or unity, in marriage. Spending a relaxed, quiet moment together allows time to reconnect and laugh together.

When our spouse sees, hears, and values our true inner person, then physical touch naturally follows. When women feel valued, they naturally feel more attractive. True fellowship stirs up our desire to caress. Nothing is more sexy than cherishing each other. Fellowship in marriage keeps the birds chirping and bees buzzing.

Laughter as an Aphrodisiac

Laughter is evidence of fellowship. Like my parents, you can weave joy throughout your marriage.

"Sometimes sex is so funny between us, we just laugh like children," a wise friend told me when I was still a newlywed. Thank heavens. Keeping it all candlelight and roses wears me out.

One secret to great sex: Romance is a balance between hard work and belly laughs. Sometimes, silliness is the best kind of relaxed sexiness. A sense of humor is a sign of intelligence. Everyone finds intelligence sexy. I can't actually prove scientifically that humor is a sign of intelligence, but I am counting on it since I am a very funny person, often accidentally.

With great tools, like humor and patience, we can relax and have more fun as lovers. It can't hurt to laugh together with tender fellowship as an aphrodisiac. If all else fails, may I suggest wearing cowboy boots to bed and nothing else? That's sure to lighten the mood. Never underestimate the power of suggestion. Sometimes just speaking a silly idea out loud super charges libido. For instance, who knows what your hubby would do if you offered him a bath towel as a superman cape?

There are times when the situation is too serious for silliness. In those cases, I am proud of you for recognizing you want more in life. I believe you have the courage you need.

Sometimes, relationships can be beyond fixing. Please seek out an objective perspective from someone with professional training, perhaps a psychologist, therapist, or clergy person. In my experience, such counselors gain vast experience by listening to people. A counselor may be able to tell you if your marriage is more normal than you realize. Some challenges are common to us all.

Even as you seek trusted counsel, remember this important truth: the relationship belongs to you. You get to decide if you are safe and satisfied staying in it while you make minor changes to create a whole new level of intimacy.

Devotion or Divorce

In our modern culture, with all its focus on sensuality, it's easy to lose the bigger picture. We may begin to believe sensuality is a substitute for tender cherishing. Physical intimacy is just a glimpse at real oneness. Ultimately, marriage is not about the sex. It's about devoted companionship that reflects God's relationship with us.

When Jesus answered the question the Pharisees asked about divorce, it's interesting to note what Jesus did not say. The Pharisees thought legal contracts and religious tradition established a marriage. Instead, Jesus reclaimed the authority about how marriage is instigated.

Jesus did not mention the courts, although He was talking to experts in Jewish and Roman law. He did not highlight the trappings of religious ceremony, although we know festive weddings were common. Some folks may have missed Jesus' point, as we all tend to do, but others did not. We want to be sure we hear His message to us today.

Jesus clarified God-designed sexual intercourse to bring two people together in marriage, the one flesh relationship. Since sex is so important, we should give it serious thought. Foreplay is only a small piece of the, ahem, action. Just like foreplay is only a small (fun) part of sexual intercourse, sex is only a small part of marriage's unique oneness.

God designed marriage to guide us into a gentle relationship, not only with our husband, but with Him. Marriage allows us to model fellowship with God for our children, if we learn to create it in our marriages. God intended for all marriages to present a picture of what unity can be like, with each other and with God. Even if we never marry, His greater intention is for all of us to experience deep fellowship with Him. Single folks have not missed out in any way. They have the opportunity to build fellowship in all their relationships.

Never Boring

Marriage can be challenging, but it's never boring. There was something so alluring about the way my mom's parents enjoyed a thousand habits of gentle affection. Their flirting was just a byproduct of the relationship they fostered. It hinted of a deeper—private and sacred—relationship. Laughter permeated their life together. Even though my mom never even thought about defining her dream marriage in a few sentences, when I asked her the question spontaneously one day, she answered immediately.

"Well, a dream marriage has to have humor."

I think she's right because I notice when Dave and I are out of sync, our sense of humor evaporates.

Like most young couples, Mom and Dad went into marriage with an almost childlike naïveté and joy. Life has a way of growing us up, though, as we soon learn. On the day my dad asked my grandparents if he could marry Mom, my grandmother Meme responded with a challenging question, "Do you promise to always make her happy?"

"I can't promise to always make her happy," replied my dad with uncanny insight, "but I promise she will never be bored!" Making fellowship a hallmark of a marriage is a lifetime process, and it's certainly not boring. Cherishing each other in tender fellowship is a reward with a bonus. Fellowship in marriage tends to spark things up.

In Case You Were Wondering...

What if we got off to the wrong start when it comes to sex? People create fun, sparky marriages all the time, even after a rough start. Jesus devoted Himself to redemption because of us. Our mistakes matter to Him. He wants to heal and comfort us.

Once we let God heal and comfort us, we find we offer healing and comfort more freely to each other. Because of past hurts we all suffer, we need tenderness in our marriages most of all.

A wise friend once told me that marriage was one long conversation. Peaceful, information-seeking marriage conversations uncover pleasing options for both spouses, circumventing long-term crisis.

In the pages that follow, we're going to get practical about how to cherish yourself, your marriage, and all your relationships. How do we have those conversational adventures that change lives? And change the dynamic in the bedroom? Believe me, you can learn the skills to change communication in your home.

Finally, you can add sparks by researching every single little bit of information you need. I like books. I believe you will giggle when you read portions of this book. Feel free to read it out loud to your hubby. Several men read this book for me throughout the publishing process. They tell me it's hilarious to read out loud with a spouse. That's a big, but nice, surprise.

We'll talk about how you can start a lifelong conversation in all aspects of life. If you can talk about sex with him, believe me, you can talk about anything. Keep reading—more adventures ahead!

Pause, Ponder, Pray, and then Proceed

Since fellowship makes great foreplay, why not rev up the spark in your marriage today?

1. Understanding your needs: How does your emotional well-being (or lack of well-being) affect your future sex life? Please pray now for God's help to enhance fellowship and humor in your life, especially in your marriage.

2. Identifying your worth: What's the most attractive thing you bring to your marriage? When are you most likely to laugh happily when you think about sexual pleasure? Your laughter is a signal to you about what you enjoy. Create a plan this week to increase your happy experiences.

3. Envisioning your future: What could you do today to honor your husband with small expressions of affection? Thank God for any small way your husband expresses his affection for you. Remember to thank him.

Whether you are married or single, focus on thanking God for small kindnesses of friends who express God's love in your life.

My prayer for you, with my love

Dear God, let this sister be honored by her husband. All women have distressing moments when we feel unmotivated and unappreciated, especially when it comes to sex. You designed physical intimacy to be a natural byproduct of fellowship in marriage. Let her bless her husband in joyful unity and laughter. Please give him eyes to see her multifaceted beauty and blessing. Let her know the lifelong companionship of true friends, including her husband, with You as her best friend. Surround her with trustworthy women who minister to her soul. Teach her to savor her own worth.

From Psalms, we declare, "My voice You shall hear in the morning, O LORD; In the morning I will direct *it* to You, And I will look up" (Psalm 5:3).

To pray for yourself

Good Father, help me know true intimacy with You. Help me bring home fellowship to my husband. Now and in the future, let me walk with You, splashing joy into all my relationships. Give me guidance about what is good, healthy, wholesome, and fun, especially when it comes to sex. In moments when I feel unappreciated, help me recognize the ways others cherish me, especially my husband. When I feel distress, show Your tenderness for me. Soothe me when my emotions get intense. Give me the awareness, self-respect, and assertiveness I need. Help me rejoice in my personal beauty, please, dear Lord. Bless me now because that's Your heart's desire. In Jesus' name. Amen.

"Many of life's failures are people who did not realize how close they were to success when they gave up." —**Thomas A. Edison**[6]

---

6   https://en.wikiquote.org/wiki/Thomas_Edison, This is presented as a statement of 1877, as quoted in *From Telegraph to Light Bulb with Thomas Edison* by Deborah Headstrom (Nashville: B&H, 2007), 22.

CHAPTER FOUR

Chosen

Why is fellowship foundational to marriage?
*Because ultimately marriage serves as a picture
of God's offer of companionship with Him.*

On a crisp fall day about nine months after our oldest daughter's wedding, I waved goodbye to the young couple after a gathering. I have no idea where the rest of the family was, but for some reason, I was alone on our driveway.

As soon as their car moved out of sight, an idea slammed me. My prayers for her had been answered beyond my imagination by a God who loves our daughter even more than I do! He knows her needs in ways I cannot hope to understand. He understood the implications of my own marriage. God knew my marriage would affect our kids' marriages. I collapsed to my knees in the driveway, and through tears, I thanked God for her husband, a blessing to our whole family.

While I did not understand my daughter's deepest needs the way God did, I still yearned for them to be met. I stood by breathlessly as God answered. Even as I write, I still cry whenever I consider God's goodness in this crucial request—that my children would marry godly people who rejoice in faith.

A healthy marriage serves as a picture of how oneness with God strengthens us and fills our life with joy. Fellowship is foundational to marriage. Yet, marriage does not come with guarantees.

Life Holds No Guarantees

Life is full of surprises, some of them pretty miserable. We may think we're mature about our faith, yet God often answers prayer in ways we do not understand. When God answers prayers, we may find ourselves humbled by His grace and generosity. For instance, looking back on my youth, I didn't deserve daughters with such strength of character, who purposefully chose such excellent mates.

Long before I met David, confusion reigned in my heart. Amazingly, my husband chose me anyway. How could someone with my background raise kids with any sense at all! Imagine my fear.

Looking back, I wasn't easy to raise. I was a creative kid who probably went undiagnosed as ADHD. My parents deserve some slack if they were bewildered about how to meet all my emotional needs. My background includes a pretty typical childhood with a few specific and tragic nuances. My sweet dad, dealing with his own childhood trauma, was an alcoholic. He spent the second half of his life sober, but as a child, I frequently felt emotionally abandoned and rejected.

By my youth, I learned to get attention any way I could, often with clever defense mechanisms. Like many young women, I quickly learned sexual forwardness garnered the attention of men. I experienced an unplanned pregnancy as a young adult. I aborted the child in a false effort to rid myself of a problem. I will share more about the ramifications of my decision in later chapters. For now, please know I am not preachy or self-righteous about how quickly life can unravel.

From my own personal experience, I understand how easily we get off course in life. We all have dear friends who turn to God in utter hopelessness when relationships tank beyond repair, often through no fault of their own. Heartbroken and filled with sorrow, these good women—mothers, mothers-in-law, sisters, wives, and daughters— could unexpectedly be us at any moment along the way.

In moments of crisis, it may seem God alone understands our pain. Or we may feel He isn't concerned about our heartache at all. However, in moments of crisis, we can experience some of the best moments of fellowship with God through prayer.

We wisely relish all the blessing of any moment, knowing life holds no guarantees. For instance, our oldest daughter, Anna, explains her choice of a mate culminated almost fifty years of prayer total. Yep, twenty-seven years of her mom-in-law's prayers combined with twenty-one of mine, not counting her grandparent's prayers. What a relief for me!

Praying for Future Spouses

Since choosing a spouse would be such a significant decision, I started praying before our kids were born. I couldn't imagine each child yet, while in my womb. I started praying for their spouses anyway. Amazingly, their choice of spouses still surprised me because God's imagination is so much bigger than mine!

Even when we devote ourselves to prayer, we have no guarantees things will turn out the way we hope. Instead, the thousands of decisions we make each day about communication either foster or erode fellowship. With so many factors, we have all the more reason to pray!

At the moment when our oldest daughter fell in love, David and I were sitting in the counselor's office each month, trying to renegotiate our marriage. As a couple, we wanted a relationship we both liked. Yet, we agreed on virtually nothing else! As Anna began planning her wedding, I marveled at her confidence. In spite of witnessing the unraveling of her parents' marriage, she chose to trust her future spouse, the man of her heart's desire.

Fearful, I imagined the worst. Would I stand on the front row of their wedding as a newly divorced mother of the bride? Would David show up with a girlfriend or, heaven forbid, a new wife? Was there any way to work through our marital issues more effectively?

Somehow our struggles to redefine our marriage, while sobering, did not necessarily make our children overly fearful. I chalk up their optimism to God's grace. Preprogramed to seek love, humans search for intimacy even when the odds conspire against us. Therefore, our kids don't necessarily mess up just because their parents' marriage got dicey. As a parent, I find this strangely comforting.

Together, a bride and groom set a new course. In God's wisdom, He blesses us with someone whose family background usually differs from our own. When Dave and I married, my heart beat with gratitude for the way he objectively analyzed my family upbringing.

An objective partner, if he is kind, can be a huge prize when it comes to understanding your family dynamics better. Even the way we talk in families can cause harm or blessing. An objective viewpoint allows us to free ourselves from bad habits. In particularly dysfunctional families, objectivity helps free us from unhealthy traditions from our childhood.

Chosen for a New Life

In fact, witnessing the difficulty in creating a healthy marriage can actually prepare our kids to press deeper for the life-giving marriage they want. A wedding is only the beginning of the fellowship God intends a couple to enjoy. But what a start!

God builds some pretty cool redemptive dynamics in the wedding process. For instance, the bride experiences a sense of being chosen. She is the beloved one—chosen by her groom. Just as God seeks us out, so she experiences the redemption and freedom of starting a new life. In fact, you often hear engaged couples say they are starting their new life together.

Having chosen a bride, the groom gains an understanding of why God chooses him. He considers the wonderful attributes of his intended and begins to understand how God sees his worthiness. The groom envisions a future with possibilities as he considers the blessing of the right wife to share life with him. The bride's willingness to trust her groom verifies his sense of leadership and worthiness.

All these redeeming, affirming processes start before the couple ever walks down the aisle or into the courthouse. As a Christian couple, both the bride and the groom have a special opportunity to understand the worth God places on His relationship with them. Understanding the worth of the other person means we will speak and act more tenderly with each other.

Defining Fellowship

In examining fellowship, let's talk about how we define it. It took me years to define fellowship as the gentle art of companionship. Your definition may be entirely different.

I was a little confused because after I became a Christian, I noticed whenever Christians said they wanted to have a fellowship, they meant a gathering. It took me awhile to figure out they meant more than a party without alcohol.

A great definition of fellowship helps us define our success at creating it in our marriage. How? A solid definition allows us to recognize fellowship when we experience the oneness we seek. Creating a good working definition helps you notice when unity wanes in your marriage. Or in any other relationships at home, church, work, or in the community.

Plus, having a good working definition of fellowship gives you words to use when you want to make changes. Additionally, to train our kids, we certainly want to pass along a clear definition to them.

Fortunately, our kids' marriages are their responsibility, not ours. This may sound silly, but I'm relieved to only work on one marriage at a time! Certainly, God wants to bless the marriages all around us, including our own, with oneness. A clear definition of fellowship moves us closer to the prize!

Today, why not gather half a dozen quotes about fellowship to print for your fridge or pin on Pinterest? By the way, wisdom often shows up in fun memes. I find my Pinterest pages multiply like formulas on a mathematician's blackboard! I invite you to join me in all the fun at https://www.pinterest.com/cathykrafve/, especially with hilarious memes about reading.

These days I wake up to a hubby who brings me coffee each morning. I love the way he obsessively checks my tire pressure, a task I invariably forget. My personal definitions go like this: "Fellowship in marriage begins with a cup of coffee." Or this: "Fellowship in my marriage cruises on fat tires." For David, his might be: "Fellowship in marriage is sharing a sense of humor." Or "The most romantic thing a couple can do together is raise kids." Maybe, like my granddaddy, yours involves bananas and cheese puffs.

You get the idea. Your definition may focus on attitudes of encouragement or time spent together, rather than thoughtful tasks, gifts, or words. To clarify practical ways of communicating love, Gary Chapman spelled out five love languages: words of affirmation, acts of service, receiving gifts, quality time, and physical touch.[7]

By creating a clear idea of what we are looking for in our own experiences of marital unity, we are empowering ourselves to savor togetherness when we experience it. We learn to ask for what we truly want. Communication improves instantly when we understand how to ask for what we want or need. That's a terrific conversation skill.

Once you have some working definitions, you begin to recognize the practical things you already do together to enhance your sense of fellowship. You can express thankfulness when your needs and wants are met. Our understanding evolves over time. Tacking down reference points for this moment in our relationship equips us to be more alert for new truths tomorrow.

Then, by cherishing each other, we feel grateful. Gratefulness blossoms into more joy and unity. Joy and unity are what we seek in all our relationships.

Gentle Companionship with God

Jesus was a joy-filled, practical philosopher who addressed the nitty-gritty of our human condition by defining marriage's beginning as sexual intercourse. One with the Creator Himself, He not only recognized humans like sex, but also acknowledged humans can be hard-hearted. His contemporaries considered Jesus a radical. In fact, even today, His teaching still changes whole cultures. Imagine the birth of freedom in a culture when many people follow Him!

---

7   Learn Your Love Language, https://www.5lovelanguages.com/, accessed 02-03-20

Thinking about the tradition of marriage in His day, no wonder folks got hot and bothered by His comments. He challenged them, as He challenges us, to give up their preconceived notion of marriage as a legal, human transaction. Instead, He asked them to embrace this truth—God established a beautiful plan for marriage, a plan beyond man-made tradition. Fortunately, when we turn to Him in prayer with our questions and challenges today, Jesus handles them as insightfully and tenderly as He handled the scholarly experts of His day.

Because God seeks us out with tenderness and respect, we freely love others. Okay, maybe that sounds a little naive. Let's face it, sometimes we love begrudgingly. We are human after all. Thankfully for us, God is perfect and faithful and unfailing in His devotion for each of us. He does not begrudge us in any way but joyfully blesses us.

God constantly chooses us, over and over again, even as we choose to push Him away frequently. His mercy toward us finds us daily, new every morning. His tender delight in us is like warm sunshine on a frosty day, bright like stars in the sky, better than puppies and kittens!

My church sings a beautiful spiritual song, expressing God's goodness in simple things we take for granted. We sing about waking up in the morning, pointed in the right direction by a God who blesses us every minute of our life. If only we were truly aware of His continuous blessing!

Outside my window as I type, I'm watching leafless limbs swaying in a gentle winter breeze. A red-breasted robin perches on my porch railing. Each season reminds us God is still present in our lives. The simplest reminder of His goodness can touch us to the core at any moment.

Tomorrow, if God wakes me again, I plan to spend the day with a beloved grandbaby. In fact, considering all He created, providing countless daily delights in our world, can there be any doubt of His tremendous love for us? He continuously provides opportunities for us to know and love Him.

Recognizing His loving presence in our life and praising Him for it is true fellowship with Him. Can there be any doubt marriage was designed by God to reflect His unfailing love, constant devotion, and joyful delight in each of us?

Quiet Conversation with God

God seeks us out by inviting us for prayer. Prayer is quiet conversation with God. In fact, if we bring prayer into our daily habits, we'll find quiet conversation spilling over into our family life as well, and into our marriage. God interacts with us in unexpected ways through prayer. While answers to prayer may seem unpredictable to us, we can count on some things about prayer to be consistent.

First, God seeks out each of us for a tender relationship. Second, He wants to hear our most heartfelt pleas and answer them. Amazingly, as we turn our burdens over to Him, we begin to notice the most unexpected daily mini-miracles. Third, our relationship with Him grows in openness and authenticity. Fourth, the gentle give-and-take of awareness and mutual respect we experience in prayer translates well into all our relationships, especially marriage.

Remember, He seeks us out and chooses us first, long before we realize He loves us. In this beautiful process of being chosen, dear one, we find fuel to nurture our own hearts. No wonder fellowship is the foundation to a healthy marriage. A good marriage offers us all a perfect picture of God's desire to be united with His people.

In Case You Were Wondering...

What if I picked the wrong person? I hear the anguish in your question. We all want to feel chosen, but often feel rejected instead.

I hope you are simply experiencing one of those minor blips on the screen all marriages endure. My prayer is that you are surrounded by trustworthy, loving friends who offer you comfort when you need it. Sometimes, we all need a weekend away to renew our appreciation for our lover.

Conversely, some of our choices prove injudicious over time. Possibly, you suffer because of poor choices, yours or his or both. If your husband acts violently toward you or is unfaithful, if he shows hostility or disrespect with his words, if his actions jeopardize the financial well-being of your family, please stay safe.

Whatever your circumstances, give yourself enough space to think clearly. You are beloved, dear to the heart of a good Father God who wants you to be safe, healthy, and victorious. You may be facing some hard decisions. With even the smallest changes today, tomorrow will be different.

Communicating your way to tender fellowship in marriage may feel like a losing battle, with more error and failure than you signed up for. No matter your marital status, you can be whole-hearted. By prayerfully choosing your own well-being, you are setting a powerful example for your children.

Pause, Ponder, Pray, and then Proceed

Oneness in marriage brings joy into our lives. Amazingly, our gratitude for God's tender affection sparks even more fellowship with all those we love.

1. Understanding your needs: When you think about being chosen as a wife, what makes you feel most joyful? Write down three blessings your husband brings to your relationship.

2. Identifying your worth: What are your best qualities? Think back on past accomplishments if need be. Considering your heart's deepest desires, what purposeful action could you take toward God's design for you, regardless of your present circumstances? Today, start enhancing one of your fabulous qualities. Write down one action point to focus on for this week. Just one thing this week—talk to a neighbor, volunteer, bake a cake, set up your easel—to spotlight your natural shininess. You can do it!

3. Envisioning your future: How could God use you to enhance fellowship in the generations after you? Please take thirty seconds right now and ask your good heavenly Father to do something wonderful for the young people in your family. Now ask Him to do the same for you. Why not? He loves you just like you love them.

My prayer for you, with my love

Dear God, please notice, with compassion, Your beautiful daughter.

Consider her heart and all that she stores there. It's so hard to be patient when we feel fed up, tired, and inadequate. Tenderly care for her anywhere she may hurt, O Lord. Teach her to love You energetically from a whole heart. Give her the joy of praying to You for those she loves, especially the future generations of her family. Please strengthen all her relationships as she courageously pursues You. Thank You, Lord.

Together, we shout out from Psalm 6:9, "The Lord has heard my supplication; The Lord will receive my prayer."

To pray for yourself

Good Father, I desperately need the joy only You can provide. I need patience where I feel fed up. Please give me energy when I feel tired. Move me from inadequate in my marriage to influential. You cherish me, but how am I supposed to know it, Lord? Especially when I feel like rejecting myself. Teach me to know my own value. Allow me to spread the glorious news that You are seeking out Your people. Teach me to strengthen my marriage so others draw near to You. I want to trust You in daily moments when things threaten to unravel. Strengthen me to choose safety for myself and my family. Please give the gift of faith to my children in spite of my own fear. Show Yourself to be strong in my life. Bless me now because that's Your heart's desire. In Jesus' name I pray. Amen.

"The more one does and sees and feels, the more one is able to do, and the more genuine may be one's appreciation of fundamental things like home, and love, and understanding companionship." —**Amelia Earhart**

CHAPTER FIVE

Super-duper Sex

Why does sex get complicated?
Because human beings are complex.
Complexity is part of our charm...

or over a year, we made our monthly trek to our counselor's office and slumped down on opposing ends of the big stuffed couch piled with pillows. He kept a stash of soft blankets and a box of tissues nearby on the end table under softly lit lamps. The Lord knows I spent enough time in this office to notice the details. After twenty years of marriage, you would think we could figure it out, but here we went again, crying and fighting in front of God and another human being.

Counseling or divorce, which was best? Unconvinced, I knew one thing for sure: talking wasn't working. We argued more than talked. Miraculously, the breakthrough moment happened in a heartbeat.

"I am only staying in this marriage for the sex," I declared defiantly. My point? There's nothing left for me in this marriage but the physical satisfaction of sex. In my mind, quite a low blow. I believe most wives would rather have great sex with their current hubby than have to start over with a new partner. Still to my way of thinking, marriage should certainly be much more than just sex.

Sex is kinda tricky for women. It's so personal it takes some practice. Maybe this is true for men too; I can only speak from what I know. My husband already knew every wrinkle and sag and remembered my body before our kids were born. If I can hardly write about this because it's so personal, imagine how much I dreaded starting over with anyone else in a sexual relationship. It takes guts to be naked with someone new. (By the way, if you have started over with someone new, I hope you give yourself credit for being courageous.)

Being polar opposites, David took my insult as a compliment. It inspired him. What man doesn't want to believe that he's such a powerhouse that his wife would hang around just for the sex? This is probably one of the more brilliant things I've ever said. When you are embroiled in, ugh, marriage counseling, it mostly feels painful and discouraging. As I made my factual but rude comment, David took heart. Here, at last, was something he was doing right.

Unsurprisingly, David began to devote attention to more success in this strategic area, which worked out great for me. And that, folks, is the story of how I fixed our marriage in one accidental comment.

If only marriage communication were that easy! Actually, it turned out to be a teeny-tiny step in a big, new direction. Still, in that moment, any hint of positive momentum amounted to a mini-miracle.

Speaking of Sex

I'm guessing we've all experienced weird moments in sexual relationships. If God designed sex, why does it have to get so complicated? If only people were simple, instead of complex! For our purposes, if I mean sexual intercourse, I will say so. Otherwise, sex refers to sexual, fun, healthy stuff.

Certainly, we all come at life with unique personalities, expectations, baggage, and insecurities. Women commonly complain about their husbands' lack of understanding and imagination when it comes to their sexual needs. For women, our sexual appetites tie intimately, irrevocably, and incessantly to our emotional needs.

Supposedly, we create intimacy together with our husbands, right? Instead, as successful women, we often feel worn out and unmotivated, especially in the sex department. Maybe not all the time, but let's say 50 percent of the time. You know, the 50 percent when we are not writing a presentation for work at midnight or wiping our adorable children's noses, or folding laundry, or driving home from church, or the million other things we do daily. So, let's talk about sex because that's really all we have the energy for. Talk.

If this is your experience, please be comforted because you are not alone. With courage we can live with intoxicating freedom and fellowship, especially in this most intimate relationship. Humans are complex, but that's part of our charm.

We must begin by taking ownership of our sexuality to come up with some strategies. Years ago, in a perfect example, a darling friend of mine shared a strategy for revving up the romance as I was about to leave with David for a road trip to beautiful South Padre beach.

"Men love junk food. Pack a picnic basket of chips and man food, you know, beef jerky. Then, buy a *Cosmo* and read it out loud all the way to the hotel. By the time you get there, his motor will be humming." From then on, when David saw *Cosmo* lying around the house, his attitude perked up. Lately, though, *Cosmo* seems kinda dull to us.

"Is it just me or is *Cosmo* starting to sound like *Seventeen* magazine," I asked Dave the last time we were driving to the beach. "Maybe their market is getting younger." Okay, maybe we're getting old. Teen quizzes and embarrassing-moment columns just don't do it for some of us.

You, too, may be craving a more elegant approach. Perhaps you have graduated to more accelerated training. If so, I have great news. Bookstore shelves are loaded with great books on the topic. But choose wisely.

We are not the only ones to notice the phenomenon of modern media's tendency to feed us rotten stuff about sex. Our culture is saturated with yucky stuff.

Sexperts of Our Own Likes and Dislikes

Thank heavens, though, one of my favorite authors, "Sexpert" Lou Paget answers all the specific questions women have when it comes to their own sexuality. Plus, she shares lots of tips on how to tactfully introduce the topic of our pleasure to our lovers. We can enhance oneness with dignity in this intimate area of our lives. Great sex starts as a great conversation. Nowhere is communicating more strategic than in the bedroom!

Lou says first, men need to "be granted the permission to ask questions about what they don't know" about sex. There may be things they don't understand from a woman's point of view.

"Second, and perhaps more important, men need to realize all women are different and therefore require different treatment. There is no possible way to know what works best for a woman without asking her."[8] May I suggest you read Lou Paget's wonderful books out loud to your lover. Very sexy.

"Finally, men need to realize that the onus of sex does not fall solely on men. Both men and women should be responsible for learning and then knowing about how to please one another. If these factors are in place, any man can become an expert lover,"[9] she adds. For your first Paget book, I recommend *How to Give Her Absolute Pleasure*, which tells a man how to please his woman.

Servant Leadership Starts at Home

Notice, I'm suggesting you focus on your pleasure first for at least five reasons.

1) As women, we often take care of ourselves last, so try going first this time.

2) If he is a good man, he's itching to please you.

3) He will relish the opportunity to learn in a very sexy, nonthreatening way.

4) Learning about your body together is hot.

5) Encouraging him to learn about you first puts him in the leadership role, which is also very hot.

---

8   Lou Paget, *How to Give Her Absolute Pleasure: Totally Explicit Techniques Every Woman Wants Her Man to Know*. (New York: Random House, 2007), Kindle locations 139–141.

9   Ibid, Kindle locations 127–131.

I am blushing. Give me a minute; I have to cool off.

Encouraging your husband to serve you is a big deal. All truly great leaders are servant leaders who understand fellowship. Yet, servant leadership seems to be a lost art in our culture. Leadership begins with the right questions.

Reading out loud together encourages your husband to serve and lead you in an area where he may respond enthusiastically to the, ahem, stimulating incentives. I pray your patience and forthright attitude will spill over with true unity in all areas of your life together.

If your husband already takes the initiative to serve your needs sexually or any other way, you are a blessed woman! Just so we are clear, starting the conversation is the hardest part. After that, it can get pretty hilarious. Pick a book or magazine you find appealing. Keep building your library so you are a "sexpert" on your own unique and wonderful sensuality.

Most importantly, if it's private, legal, safe, and honoring, never fail to try something new. Ask him to talk to you about his new ideas. This kind of unified fellowship nurtures fun. You may find your spouse dreams of something sweet and easy to fulfill. Most of the time fantasies are not actually as romantic in reality as in imagination, but often they are pretty hilarious. Sex does not have to be so intensely serious; it's supposed to be fun.

Communicating Our Way to Satisfying Intimacy

Women get so busy serving everyone else, we lose track of ourselves. For instance, Dave and I hit the rough spot at the twenty-year mark. When the kids leave home, rough spots turn out to be fairly common, but who knew? Therefore, I sought out a trusted friend. She sat across the table and looked deeply into my eyes the way only a truly good friend can.

"I need someone who knows me well and remembers who I was before David," I told her on the day we met for lunch. I knew she would comfort me and offer insight.

"Are you positive he is not cheating on you, Cathy?" she asked me gently.

"Yes, I know for sure he is not," I said emphatically.

"How can you know for sure? Men do it all the time," she insisted tenderly. I am sure I sounded naïve.

"Because he knows he will never have better sex." We laughed pretty hard. Yep, she's known me a long time. Her longstanding, loyal friendship always reminds me of my youth when I dared to be vulnerable and adventurous. I took chances back then. I spoke up. Her encouragement meant so much to me that day when I momentarily forgot who I was.

We never want to create the impression that somehow a wife can or should co-dependently overcompensate by trying to ensure a husband's faithfulness. I like what author, pastor, and counselor Chris Legg says on this topic, "It is my job to not cheat, not my wife's job to keep me from cheating."[10] I hope you will look for more of Chris's practical insight on dozens of family and marriage topics, including, for instance, how to handle it when a husband is too demanding about sex.

God-Given Free Will

Plainly, many women may try the mind-blowing sex method in marriage and still their husbands may cheat. Naturally, individuals with God-given free wills make decisions, including heartbreaking ones sometimes. Because humans are complex, we can be very messy.

I'm not advocating staying in a marriage if your spouse cheats. Those moments are so personal, only you can decide what to do next. The rest of us should shut up and refrain from judging. There's no way we can begin to comprehend everything happening behind closed doors in someone else's marriage. All I'm saying is if you are married, do everything you can to enjoy great sex. But great sex depends on great communication.

Sexual adventures can be tricky. Sex should be fun for both people involved. It should be safe and legal. Discomfort for either spouse is the trigger to stop and talk. Ask each other specific questions to spur true communication. Is the sexual encounter fun, safe, legal, private, and honoring to each other? If it's in the comfort zone for both of you, have fun.

---

10   Chris Legg, From a personal email when asked for his wisdom for this book. 12-10-20. Used by permission.

Sometimes we must reestablish intimacy by tenderly affirming each other. Anytime conversation prompts you to restate your commitment to each other for the long haul, that's going to be good for all aspects of intimacy. Then, there's the problem of porn and it's proven threat to intimacy.

The Problem with Porn

Without being prudish, as Christian women, we need to be aware of the scientifically established dangers of porn. In her book *Fight for Love*, Rosie MaKinney lists truths about porn, the resulting problems, and offers footnotes to back up her conclusions with scientific studies.[11] Here are a few:

Porn creates dissatisfaction in and out of the bedroom.[12]

Porn destroys authenticity and intimacy.[13]

Porn highjacks the brain, creating addictive thought pathways.[14]

Porn teaches that women are aroused by verbal and physical abuse.[15]

Children who live in homes with porn consumption have a greater risk of accidental porn exposure.[16]

Fellowship is the foundation of (porn) recovery.[17]

Rosie challenges the way women are taught to be codependent when it comes to pornography. She emphasizes that early intervention is the best response. I keep extra copies of Rosie's book on my shelf to hand off to friends whenever the topic of porn comes up.

Even so-called soft porn can have a raw edge. With discipline, you can train your gut to recognize the difference. For instance, some things are scary, uncomfortable, illegal, unsafe, unhealthy, or they may impose on or hurt innocent bystanders. I cannot overstate the deceit of porn. Anything feeling raw or disrespectful may disrupt fellowship between you two.

---

11   Rosie MaKinney, *Fight For Love* (Nashville: B&H Publishing, 2020) 9.
12   Ibid, 12.
13   Ibid, 13.
14   Ibid, 19-28.
15   Ibid, 129.
16   Ibid, 162.
17   Ibid, 53.

Someone always gets cheated with porn. No matter the lies you hear, please disregard the myth of consenting adults or innocent bystanders. One of my favorite ways to evaluate a decision is with this saying: "If God is in it, everyone gets a blessing." With porn, someone always gets hurt, even if it's the "consenting" adult actors.

Sex Was God's Good Idea

Put it another way and it becomes crystal clear. Can God be in porn? Absolutely not. We have to recognize the enemy of our soul will hijack any good thing God creates if we let him, even sex. Especially sex. Since sex goes straight to God's long-term plan for our lives and our families, the enemy offers us a counterfeit.

Don't forget, sex was God's good idea in the first place. Believe me when I say, I'm not the least bit judge-y about sex. God created sexuality as a blessing, a way of creating oneness for a couple. In contrast, porn divides. In this modern age, we are all constantly confronted by porn in a steady stream of subtle or not-so-subtle social media assaults.

We all know dear friends who've claimed victory from porn addiction. As they courageously speak up, they offer a path to freedom for us all. Their invaluable insight affords us a clue about how they won ongoing victory. Victory means more intimacy and freedom.

Creating intimacy in your marriage includes talking about sex in vulnerable and wholehearted ways. You have a free will, so choose great sex with your spouse because you can. I say leave nothing on the table when it comes to sex. Whatever you do, don't miss out on the childlike wonder, tenderness, and fellowship that develops when sex becomes a lifelong expression of love, delight, and tenderness.

In Case You Were Wondering...

Why isn't porn okay; it's not like he's having sex with anyone else, right? Just like when we take a wrong turn on a vacation, porn is a quick way to get lost. Porn diverts a person's attention away from their spouse and consequently away from their family's best interests. Many women ask, "Why porn and why not me?"

Media sources promote porn's unrelenting pressure, saturating our culture in what can only be described as cruel and unusual punishment. All people are increasingly in danger of suffering porn addiction, especially our children and grandchildren.

"So, I did early intervention inadvertently. Early intervention is exactly the right thing to do," Rosie said when I interviewed her on Fireside Talk Radio.[18]

Dave Howe, in his book *Live Pure and Free,* written specifically for men, touches on the pain there can be around the topic of intimacy.

"I was hiding from God," Dave writes. "I was moving farther away from Him, but at the same time, I was desperately worried that He would just abandon me."[19]

Especially in our churches and homes, women need to join together to call porn what it is, a shortcut to danger. We can stand together non-judgmentally in holding each other accountable. By seeking professional counseling and great resources, we address porn as a serious threat to families.

In contrast, fun, healthy, respectful sexual moments in marriage stimulate fellowship because they are so private and special. My prayer is that you will courageously talk to your spouse in tender conversations about sex, increasing your pleasure and trust in this crucial part of your relationship.

Pause, Ponder, Pray, and then Proceed

Fellowship and sex are intrinsically related for women. Please help your husband understand this. The following questions are designed to get your own creative juices flowing, so you will be a confident woman. Confidence comes from knowing what is true and doing what is hard.

---

18 *Fireside Talk Radio,* Rosie MaKinney, "Porn-proofing Your Kids," https://cathykrafve.com/porn-addiction/, accessed 1-28-2021.
19 Dave Howe, *Live Pure and Free* (Minneapolis: Tristan Publishing, 2017), 78.

For many women, the hard part is talking about sex. But confident women are sexy.

1. Understanding your needs: What new strategy are you willing to introduce to cherish your lover? Today, make a list of things you could say to talk about sex. When it comes to sex, what puts your heart at peace? Add those special peaceful thoughts to your list to talk about with your hubby.

2. Identifying your worth: Which paragraph of a good book could you read out loud hilariously to your lover for further stimulating discussion? (I certainly hope this book makes the cut!) Think of three wholesome, new ideas you might want to try in the bedroom. It's okay if they feel a little risqué or silly.

3. Envisioning your future: Since physical intimacy is the picture of emotional and spiritual intimacy, what can you do to make sex more joyful? If porn addiction is part of your current situation, who can you trust to hold you accountable? How do you plan to seek change? If fear and failure were not a part of the scenery, what would be the deepest yearnings of your heart when it comes to increasing the intimacy in your marriage? I pray you find the courage to talk about this important and intimate topic.

My prayer for you, with my love

Dear God, You are the One who designed all creation and gave us the ability to form a union and procreate. Please bless my sister with renewed wonder in her sexuality. What a miracle! Lord, it's easy to feel defeated and depleted, especially in something as intimate as sex. Bless Your beautiful daughter with a tenderness for her own body, a temple for Your glory. Please let her husband rejoice in her love. May she rejoice in her relationship with him, tenderly relishing their sexual expression of love for each other.

Together we ask You to receive our praise from Psalm 9: "I will praise *You*, O LORD, with my whole heart; I will tell of all Your marvelous works. I will be glad and rejoice in You; I will sing praise to Your name, O Most High" (Psalm 9:1–2).

To pray for yourself

Good Father, thank You for giving me a body I can enjoy. Thank You for designing my skin to respond to touch. Teach my heart to tremble with gratitude for the freedom and fun You intend me to enjoy sexually. When I feel defeated and unable to think about sex, help my heart rise in triumph to enjoy the privilege of physical intimacy. When I feel depleted, enrich our marriage as a source of fun and wonder. Help us claim freedom from all distracting counterfeits, like porn. Give me words to express my desires to my husband. Help me put lots of creativity into sex. Let us consider the wonders You designed and rejoice with You at the marvels of Your creation! Strengthen us in faithful devotion to each other and to You. Bless me now because that's Your heart's desire. In Jesus' name. Amen.

"Humans love sex, we need sex, it's how we connect, it reminds us we're alive, it's the third most basic human need, after food and good movie popcorn." —**Billy Crystal**

CHAPTER SIX

Disney and Fairy Dust

Why does divorce happen?
Because human hearts can be hard, rather than whole.

The whole town showed up for our wedding. Friends and family packed the beautiful Lutheran sanctuary. For David, doing anything in front of a crowd foreshadowed how much my introverted husband loves me. Guests enjoyed an extra-long ceremony, all the verses of several hymns, and any falderal I could think up. The pastor pronounced us man and wife, probably with a sigh of relief. We ran down the aisle, smiling and holding hands.

Dad arranged for his big, burly friend to whisk us away to the reception. A larger-than-life character who treated every vehicle like a race car, Jim built a business repossessing cars. You never wondered what Jim thought, another thing my dad liked about his friend.

We raced to the reception in Dad's tricked-out Ford van, assured of a fast start to our marriage. The van, a vagabond left over from the '70s, sported a mini-fridge and shag carpeting. One summer, my parents installed a fold-out bed for a camping trip to Yellowstone, but thankfully, the mattress was stashed away on our wedding day. Nope, there was nothing socially rigid about my dad.

Joyfully, we leaped into our getaway van. My wedding dress festooned around us like icing on the cake. My handsome groom looked better than any cake topper I ever saw. In our first quiet moment I said something totally inappropriate to my dashing new spouse.

"Now I understand why people get divorced."

From the front seat, Jim declared, "I can't believe you just said that to your new husband!"

Suddenly, the reality of keeping my commitment for the next fifty years slammed me. Hollywood had lied to me! I guess I thought Walt Disney was going to show up at the altar and sprinkle fairy dust all over us. People live together fifty plus years without the help of magic. But the feeling in the pit of my stomach reminded me how selfish I can be.

Recently, I asked David if he remembered that moment. He said no.

"I am pretty sure I had other stuff on my mind," he laughed.

David already knew his young bride well enough to absorb the shockingly true things I tend to say, even in those first few minutes of our marriage. Or maybe he just failed to listen. Either way, my comment didn't faze him. Like Jesus, David has a knack for cutting through to what matters.

The Truth About Divorce

When it comes to divorce, we must speak truthfully and cut through to what matters. Jesus cut through to the shockingly simple truth when the Pharisees challenged Him about marriage and Moses' command. Was divorce permissible?

"They said to Him, 'Why then did Moses command to give a certificate of divorce, and to put her away?'" (Matthew 19:7).

In His response, Jesus immediately snuffed out any confusion about paperwork and man-made legalities. "He said to them, 'Moses, because of the *hardness of your hearts,* permitted you to divorce your wives, but from the beginning it was not so. And I say to you, whoever divorces his wife, except for sexual immorality, and marries another, commits adultery; and whoever marries her who is divorced commits adultery" (verses 8–9, emphasis mine).

At its root, divorce is not about the paperwork, although we still get tripped up by all the legal maneuverings. Instead, hard hearts cause divorce, as Jesus taught us. Fortunately, fellowship is the cure. Fellowship in marriage results when two hearts commit to stay tender over the course of a lifetime. Think of the miracle Jesus exposed with His words! Jesus clearly stated divorce happens because of hard hearts. He said so right after emphasizing the one flesh truth. According to Jesus' straightforward assessment, divorce has nothing to do with legal maneuvering. In fact, for instance, divorce can happen behind the scenes when one of the spouses initiates another marriage by having sexual intercourse with someone else. In today's world, we call that cheating.

If only we thought through all the ramifications of Jesus' simple, clear words on the topic of marriage. For instance, because we don't acknowledge the one flesh relationship as the instigating act of marriage, we say the spouse cheated by having sexual intercourse with someone else. In fact, they've initiated another marriage relationship. Confusing? You bet!

Because our culture disregards what Jesus said about marriage and divorce, we can easily fail to give people the credit they deserve when they salvage damaged marriages. We often fail to acknowledge the inevitable fallout and heart break for all concerned whenever cheating interrupts a marriage. We burden wronged spouses with false guilt when we should be supporting them in their decisions following their heartbreak.

Fellowship: Hard Heart Prevention

Fellowship is a cheating prevention plan.

We should be clear when we talk about divorce, in the church particularly. When most folks get to the courthouse, the divorce is long past. For many women, one of the hardest moments comes when they are forced to file the divorce papers because the husband refused to do so.

By Jesus' definition, if cheating happens, divorce has already taken place because another marriage is initiated by having sexual intercourse with someone new.

For instance, if the husband has cheated on a wife, he has already initiated a new marriage. His old one is dissolved because he cheated. He may beg his grieving wife to give him another chance to repair their original marriage. Restoration may be the best—if extremely difficult—option, particularly if kids are involved.

Based on Jesus' teaching, I believe she is free to decide what comes next. If the husband postpones resolution as he continues his new relationship, he forces his injured wife to file for legal divorce. Forcing her to file the legal documents adds insult to injury. Sadly, the cheating spouse, especially in church it seems, will often play for our sympathy by saying the other spouse filed.

I sympathize with anyone who has been through a divorce for any reason. Certainly, I know how awful it feels when your marriage unravels. But the truth about divorce is not in who filed the paperwork at the courthouse. Instead of falling for that old line, let's take a careful look at what Jesus said.

If we believe marriage ends when one of the spouses has sexual intercourse with someone else, we must face significant repercussions of our belief. When we understand Jesus' teaching, we acknowledge once cheating occurs the faithful spouse is free. Because a new marriage has been initiated, the first one ends. In the church, we need to include this basic practical premise in our thinking in order to respect what Jesus taught.

Significantly, we all know amazing marriages that somehow miraculously survive cheating. With honor, we can applaud the courage and fortitude it takes to rebuild trust and fellowship after such a betrayal. Especially for the sake of any children, we must join with those couples in full support and encouragement for their sacrifice, unselfishness, and authenticity.

We need to understand many people are wounded when a spouse is unfaithful. Whenever someone goes outside marriage for sexual intercourse, the two spouses are injured, plus any other people who enter into sexual relationships with the cheating spouse. Someone will inevitably be abandoned and injured no matter how the story turns out. Humans are messy due to our free will decisions to make selfish choices. To be healthy ourselves, we must recognize our own messiness and reach out with compassion to others, no matter their circumstances.

Decision Makers

A healthy reference point empowers us for healthy relationships. Too many women stay in hopeless, even dangerous, marriages. Divorce may not be the happily-ever-after fairy-tale ending we crave. But perceiving divorce as rejection and failure could be dangerous when in fact divorce may be safety and health. Sadly, legal divorce may be by far the best survival choice for physical safety and essential mental health in many cases. Certainly, we don't have to avoid legal divorce to our own injury or the injury of our children, especially if the other spouse has already initiated another relationship.

Sometimes divorce is giving up too soon. But sometimes it's the only heartbreaking, yet healthy and necessary choice.

Jesus puts the responsibility squarely on the husband when talking to the Pharisees—the male leadership of the day. "He said to them, "Moses, because of the hardness of your hearts, permitted you to divorce your wives, but from the beginning it was not so. And I say to you, whoever divorces his wife, except for sexual immorality, and marries another, commits adultery; and whoever marries her who is divorced commits adultery" (Matthew 19:8–9).

He clearly stated that whoever divorces *his wife* commits adultery unless the wife has already had sexual intercourse with someone else. So, at the same moment, Jesus acknowledged women are decision makers too when it comes to sex. By acknowledging the wife might choose to be involved in "sexual immorality," He indicates her decisions shift responsibility to her.

The word Jesus used for immorality is πορνεια (porneia).[20] Looks familiar doesn't it? Πορνεια gets translated as fornication, rather than sexual immorality, in many English translations. It's a fascinating word with clear historical parameters sometimes lost in English. Here's a sample from my favorite lexicon: "In other words, sexual intercourse

---

20 Matthew 19:9, *The New Greek English Interlinear New Testament,* Translators: Robert Brown et al, Editors: Kurt Aland et al.

of a married man with an unmarried woman would usually be regarded as πορνεια 'fornication,' but sexual intercourse of either an unmarried or married man with someone else's wife was regarded as adultery, both on the part of the man as well as the woman."[21] The other word used, μοιχ- (moix-), commonly translates as adultery.[22] Phew, that's complicated. Let me offer my simple thoughts.

No Double Standards

If, like me, you've been scratching your head about the difference between fornication and adultery, guess what? There's a good reason for our confusion. The same confusion still exists when translators try to create a Bible translation in any new language. In fact, the confusion only clears up if we understand how Jesus defined marriage. His explanation about sexual intercourse initiating marriage clears up all the confusion.

Jesus was talking to a generation who believed, perhaps like many people today, if a married man had sexual intercourse with an unmarried woman, well, maybe not such a big deal, only fornication. If any man had sexual intercourse with a married woman, they considered it adultery. Instead of adhering to the traditional explanations, Jesus told the leaders if a wife cheats, the husband is free to remarry without being concerned about committing adultery. This seems like an odd response unless we dig deeper. Why did Jesus respond the way He did? Because He spelled out clearly that divorce took place when either spouse has consensual sexual intercourse with someone else.

Jesus kept it simple. He cut right through the cultural nuances and confusion and eliminated any double standard. In fact, He ignored the confusion of labels like adultery or fornication. You can always tell when someone is being legalistic; they will try to justify their bad behavior with technicalities. Actually, labels serve to grade the seriousness of the offense, thereby downgrading the injustice inflicted. Those

---

21 *Greek-English Lexicon of the New Testament Based on Semantic Domains,* Volume 1, Johannes P. Louw and Eugene A. Nida, (New York, United Bible Societies, 1988, 772
22 Ibid.

confusing labels dilute attention from the real issue: a broken commitment. Imagine how the unfailing God feels about unfaithfulness!

Modern readers may have a hard time understanding Jesus' words even now. We are often still burdened with some of the same false cultural nuances handed down through centuries. In our culture today, we tend to call it cheating anytime anyone leaves one sexually engaged relationship for another without verbally or legally breaking off the first commitment.

As an old person, I find the whole topic kind of confusing. I never know when young people tell me they're dating, if they mean they are sleeping together. Plus, I don't think it's any of my business, so I'm afraid to ask for clarity. But, oh my, how confusing! Interestingly, the younger generation's perspective may closely resemble the truth Jesus is sharing, perhaps more so than some of the traditional teaching.

Some folks experienced shock at Jesus' straightforward answers. However, He puts our minds at rest with practical information. I love the way He clarified that divorce is not about rules but about relationship. We divorce because our hearts become hard. Simple.

Legal divorce, dissolving the pact made at the courthouse with a marriage license, is merely the final step in an outcome for a relationship already in crisis for a while, even if one spouse was unaware.

Fostering Fellowship

Since hard hearts presage divorce, we should definitely take a moment to think about how to diagnose a hard heart. Especially our own, since our own heart is the only one we have any control over! Why do our hearts get too worn out to try anymore?

We may feel tired of trying to foster fellowship with a husband. Feelings of rejection may factor in, even if they are only imagined. That means it's easier for us to develop habits of harshness, rather than gentleness. (Fortunately, good communication strategies offer hope for many marriages. I'll spell out some great strategies in later chapters of this book.)

Perhaps, we think we know the prescribed outcome of every argument, so we quit talking. Fear may create a crust on our hearts because we get tired of hurting. The crust becomes a shell, then hardens into a wall.

Before we know it, we may feel trapped and alone. How do we break free? Can we lead others to freedom? Wholeheartedness is the goal for our marriage and life.

Hard-hearted or Wholehearted

Wholeheartedness is the opposite of hard-heartedness. We close our hearts because we feel wounded and hurt. When we begin to heal and experience wholeheartedness, our hearts can open back up. This process of closing and opening back up reminds me of the daylilies growing in my garden. Each day, in the warm sunlight, they display their brilliant orange glow. In the cool of the evening, though, they close tightly. In our homes, we want to create enough warmth so our hearts shine brilliantly day or night.

If hurt causes hearts to harden and close, can we restore openness and joy? Brené Brown designated an open-hearted way of living as wholeheartedness, as opposed to broken heartedness. She wrote about collecting the stories of people who seemed to have a joyful life regardless of their circumstances.

"I wanted to look at these stories as a whole, so I grabbed a Sharpie and wrote the first word that came to my mind on the tab: Wholehearted. I wasn't sure what it meant yet, but I knew that these were stories about people living and loving with their whole heart."[23]

Anyone can have a hard heart, but how do we choose wholeheartedness when our hearts are broken? One of the worst side effects of divorce is the permeating sense of humiliation accompanying it, the sense of inescapable public shame. The trick is to have a whole heart, even when it's bruised. Even when you feel your best option means going ahead and carrying the divorce papers to the courthouse with your head held up.

---

23 Brené Brown, *The Gift of Imperfection* (Center City, Minnesota: Hazeldon Publishing, 2010), x.

Brené uncovered a list of adjectives that helps us get a bead on what we target for our lives. "The *Do* column was brimming with words like worthiness, rest, play, trust, faith, intuition, hope, authenticity, love, belonging, joy, gratitude, and creativity. The *Don't* column was dripping with words like perfection, numbing, certainty, exhaustion, self-sufficiency, being cool, fitting in, judgment, and scarcity."[24] The contrast makes it obvious which column we want to adopt for the health of our own hearts.

I love the way she shared her personal epiphany in the preface to all the good information she offers in the pages that follow: "For me, believing was seeing. I believed first, and only then I was able to see how we can truly change ourselves, our families, and our communities. We just have to find the courage to live and love with our whole hearts."[25]

A wife may suffer through a marriage when a husband is emotionally absent but making demands of her. We need to give hope to each other. Can a woman find her way back to a whole heart? Of course. Many women—maybe all—have their hearts broken along the way. Yet, we all know women who courageously and victoriously raise their heads and healed hearts to offer hope to others. Sometimes, for reasons of their own, women make courageous decisions to hang in there.

Even when a marriage continues to be less than what she wants, a wife can learn to nurture herself and her own heart. She can turn to God and to those He provides to find comfort and support for her decisions. Plus, she can make small changes in her own behavior. Even small changes will impact the dynamics of marriage communication.

It's so easy to give up on fellowship, to let our hearts become hard. Choosing wholeheartedness feels like an impossible miracle. When we feel like our marriage is crashing down on us, we are tempted to bury ourselves, hiding in a rubble of despair and grief.

For some, though, divorce morphs into the start of their own happily ever after. Climbing out of the wreckage of a failed marriage is not for wimps. It's for warrior women who know what they want for themselves and for their children—whole hearts, not broken ones. Whole-

---

24 Ibid, x
25 Ibid, xv

heartedness is for those who turn to a mighty God, letting Him be strong in our weakest, most sacred places.

Wholehearted and Worthy of Love

All women struggle to believe we are worthy of love, especially if our marriage suffers any kind of crisis. Sister, you are not alone in this. Blessedly, sometime around the age of fifty there seems to be a moment when women talk about getting comfortable in our own skin. So, there's hope.

Seriously, though, depending on your age, fifty may seem like a long way off. (Or, in my case, a long time ago!) No matter our age, we may hate to admit we feel needy. Neediness is not popular in our modern culture of powerful, successful women. However, all humans feel a little needy sometimes. It's okay to admit it. In fact, neediness might be the glue holding us together sometimes.

Our innate desire for companionship—our neediness, if you will—drives us to pursue a closer relationship with a spouse, for instance. With our friends. Or, more importantly, with God.

As women, we are under attack by an enemy who wants us to feel so brokenhearted we are of no use in God's kingdom. Satan knows full well God uses the weak to display His strength. Therefore, Satan takes a huge tactical risk in the battle. Tempting us, our enemy gambles we will go bitter.

If we trust God, though, He empowers us in our most wounded place, our broken heart. Too bad for the enemy. Instead, we claim our position as warrior women, under the care of God, the Great Physician of our souls, who makes our hearts whole again. Instead of bitterness, the discipline of joy shines in our lives.

When a marriage inevitably falters, as all marriages do at times, our neediness drives us to a more intimate relationship with God. Whether in sorrow or joy, God offers us our best hope of true unfailing love. Whether you are rebooting your marriage or your life, He offers healing for wounded, broken hearts. Jesus went before us, so we could find the path leading to wholeheartedness.

You are exceptionally prepared and designed to be successful in the purpose for which God created you. Like a computer preprogrammed to boot up, you are pre-designed for success in your marriage because God designed you. Having exceptional preparation and design doesn't make the task easy, though.

Truly, while you may not know until you get there, divorce may be an unavoidable part of your future. For some, divorce unfolds as an inescapable consequence of hard heartedness, even if you cultivate wholeheartedness for yourself.

To develop the skills you need for successful relationships, implement small new communication strategies in the personal test lab of your own home. Create fellowship in every aspect of your life, particularly if you think marriage may be part of your future. Please choose today to live to your fullest potential as you intentionally apply all your natural creativity.

Just to be clear, women tell me all the time they struggle along the way even in the best marriages. But pay attention to your gut. Make the small changes—or the big ones—you need to make in order to stay healthy.

In Case You Were Wondering...

Will my divorce affect any hope of a good future? No matter your experience, even divorce one or more times, there is hope of a great future for you. Do you believe God is the God of second chances? We all know many divorced people who create truly exceptional second or third marriages.

Those creative folks share some common traits. First, they truthfully take responsibility for the decisions they made leading up to divorce. Second, without blaming their ex, they limit their responsibility to their own decisions. Third, they go through the divorce process humbly with their kids, trying to spare them as much pain as possible. Finally, when they claim the opportunity to remarry, they do so wholeheartedly with joy, gratitude, and determination. Plus, it doesn't hurt to get lots of folks praying.

No matter how hurt you may feel today, please know that God has a bright future for you, with or without marriage. There is freedom in pursuing God's plan for you. In fact, being free to serve God and others unencumbered may be the silver lining following divorce.

Like a daylily, our hearts can open again brilliantly. This truth may feel impossible to believe but believe it anyway. Our failures or traumas do not limit God. He constantly makes a way for us in ways beyond our imagination. I want you to know that I believe in your bright and brilliant future.

Pause, Ponder, Pray, and then Proceed

We often feel our days are so hectic we can't take a moment for ourselves. When a heart feels broken, we owe it to ourselves to take the time we need to grieve and reflect. In my own experience, particularly surrounding my abortion, grief resurfaces unexpectedly, even as I experience healing along the way. I completely embrace God's forgiveness and love for me. Yet, just when I think my heart is whole, another old wound surfaces.

1. Understanding your needs: Today, you could make a list of wounds in your heart and then burn the list. Or write them on a seashell and throw it far into the ocean to be washed away forever. But those things will only work if you let go of these wounds and present them to God to heal. Which trustworthy friend seems to be sent from God to comfort you in this moment?

2. Identifying your worth: Speaking of becoming wholehearted, for the next thirty days, which adjectives best describe your habitual heart attitude? Which attributes could you share as affirmations in the lives of those around you? When our hearts are broken, it's hard to recover. Sharing affirmations with others will help you see the value God puts on you, too.

3. Envisioning your future: How would you feel today if you picked one new positive adjective and practiced adding it into the way you think about yourself? I love the word *exceptional* for you. In what ways are you beautifully exceptional?

My prayer for you, with my love

Dear God, You are the One who designed each of us to be exceptional. This beautiful sister brings her own broken heart to You for mending. We stand in Your presence. Is it any wonder she may feel combative and demeaned, facing down a trauma like divorce, Lord? Teach her to grab ahold of Your perspective on her worthiness. Alert her heart today to the little love gifts You are sending her way in a child's whisper, in a bright moonbeam, in the comfort of a friend, in the soft moans of an unspoken prayer. Lord, grant us whole hearts, we pray!

Together, we declare with the psalmist: "The LORD also will be a refuge for the oppressed, A refuge in times of trouble. And those who know Your name will put their trust in You; for You, LORD, have not forsaken those who seek You" (Psalm 9:9–10).

To pray for yourself

Good Father, You advocate for me when my marriage feels like it's crumbling. You keep on advocating for my family. When I feel combative, help me claim receptivity, for Your name's sake. When others demean me, remind me that You honor me. You demonstrate Your esteem for me in surprising ways. You trust me with the hardest situations and strengthen me for challenges. I am exceptional because You made me in Your image and You are exceptional. You alone are the Holy One. I am Your servant, Your ambassador, Your royal daughter. Bless me now because that's Your heart's desire. In Jesus' name. Amen.

"When you understand your own uniqueness, you don't compete or conspire against others, you celebrate them!" —SharRon Jamison

CHAPTER SEVEN

Best Christmas Ever

Why is fun so underrated?
*Because most folks don't realize fun
is just as spiritual as hard work.*

my dad was a master fun-creator. His leadership in the dynamics of fun caused spontaneous combustion in our family, igniting fellowship in our lives.

He gave our family a beautiful gift when I was in high school.

My parents intended to take us snow skiing in Colorado for Christmas one year before my siblings and I grew up and left for college. They planned for nearly a year, saving for such an extravagant holiday. A white Christmas? Texans find it hard to picture!

Imagine how shocked and overwhelmed we were when Mom's dad died suddenly of a heart attack a few months before our trip. Thinking back, we all assumed he would die a long, slow death of emphysema, since he had a horrible cough. Like so many in his generation, he smoked cigarettes excessively, addicted before he realized the danger.

With his death, all the excitement drained out of our Christmas plans. We felt we should be thankful because the trip was very special. Secretly, though, we dreaded leaving Meme alone. Why couldn't we just stay home with her, we wondered privately, drooping under our grief.

Imagine our delight when Dad announced a special Christmas surprise for our whole family. Before we left the DFW airport, he arranged for Meme to receive a plane ticket to come join us in a few days.

"I've done my part, the rest is up to her," he concluded.

Surprises, Suspense, and Pure Joy

Suspense tickled our imagination as we waited to see what she would decide. Meme had never been on an airplane.

The Wright brothers flew their plane in 1903, only a few years before Meme was born in 1912. They probably still gave newspaper interviews in her childhood. Meme was just a girl in 1927 when Charles Lindbergh soloed across the Atlantic Ocean for the first time in human history.

As a young married woman, she could remember when it looked like the Germans would win WWII because they had superior air power. That is, until American men and women helped the war effort by building American airplanes in American factories all over the US.

Then, in the 1960s, I remember Meme and Granddaddy being disappointed when the original Fort Worth airport gave way to shiny new DFW. Yet, she had never flown herself. Maybe she didn't trust such a new-fangled invention.

Anxiously, we waited, wondering if our courageous Meme would fly all the way to Colorado by herself to be with us. And, get this—she'd never seen powder snow. Her first act after settling in at the hotel was to plop down in the soft snow and swish it around with her arms to make a snow angel, laughing hilariously.

Mom decorated our rooms with twinkle lights and sparkling ornaments. We spent evenings in front of a glowing fire, watching snowflakes fall gently outside frosty windows. Lighthearted, Meme laughed about everything. She knew she was loved, and she was happy in spite of losing her one true love only a few months before.

Fun Group Dynamics in Families

Kind thoughtfulness and surprises were so natural to Dad, yet he would never have bothered with a fancy word like fellowship. His willingness to make a special place for his mom-in-law in our family vacation made it fun for us all. Together, we drank hot chocolate and sang "Jingle Bells" in a sleigh pulled by sturdy horses. Dad understood cherishing each other by having fun together in life's crucial moments.

Fun contributes significantly to group dynamics. In our devotion to spirituality, we may miss the following six truths about fun.

- Many people don't realize fun is just as spiritual as hard work.
- Fun creates a way to focus on each other, enjoying the time spent together with no agenda. Fun is a gift we give each other.
- Fun gives us a microcosm of eternity, when time pressures no longer exist.
- Fun gets a bad rap because many people assume fun fosters self-focus. In fact, the opposite is true. Like my dad, those who have the most fun in life master the unselfish art of making life enjoyable for everyone else.
- Fun lets us enjoy a little recreation. Our sorrows and life's distractions can weigh us down until we forget to relax. Yet, Jesus often rested, especially in moments with His closest friends.
- Fun is *not* always spontaneous and free. Often fun happens because of the thoughtful, sacrificial act of a giver, like my dad.

Sadly, we may view fun like the orphan child of the spiritual world. Why? Because having fun together requires communication and communication can be hard work!

We all know naturally gifted people who clown around, lightening any task with humor and a joyful spirit. But clowning around only goes so far; it can even get on others' nerves after a while. Therefore, one of the most crucial communication skills to develop in marriage includes researching each other's preferences. Whether we talk about fun, sex, parenting, or almost any topic, communication skills take hard work. Yep, hard work sounds like the opposite of fun!

My dad instinctively perceived the mood of our family that Christmas and took action. Crossroads in life sometimes surprise us. We can find ourselves exhausted when a loved one dies, for instance. Especially in marriage, even the most naturally fun person gets weary.

Fun Inventories

Sometimes, we may need to relax and have some fun even if it feels like a sacrifice. In just such a moment, a dear friend happened to hand me and David a terrific book, *His Needs, Her Needs* by Willard F. Harley, Jr.

I liked the whole book, but a lightbulb of understanding lit up for us when we got to the back of the book. By *we*, I mean I read the whole book, I took the test, I realized it was awesome, I photocopied a blank test for David, and I handed it to him to take, too. Then I sat there while he took the test. All the while, I acted like it was a totally fun thing to do together. I'm guessing Dave took the test because if he hadn't I might have forced him to read the whole book!

By test, I mean the Recreational Enjoyment Inventory in the back of the book. Basically, Recreational Enjoyment Inventory[26] lists entertaining activities my husband and I never thought to do together. Taxidermy and ham radio made the list. (We still haven't tried those.)

While we both love live music and dining out, we discovered only one of us thought anything educational was fun. Wow, what a revelation! In fact, as I write I realize David and I need to review the list again because grandchildren change everything fun. There's a potter's wheel in our garage to prove it.

Make Up Your Own Fun Inventory

Knowing your personal idea of fun together keeps you from getting led astray by well-meaning people. For instance, folks will tell you that each of your children needs a unique extracurricular activity. However, modern people live such full-throttle lifestyles in this age of two-income families, children may simply need downtime. Downtime helps preserve our relationships.

---

26 Willard F. Harley, Jr., *His Needs, Her Needs: Building an Affair-Proof Marriage* (Grand Rapids,: Revell, 1986), 208–213.

Reconnecting Over Recreation

Couples need to reconnect over recreation, even if the thought of planning something seems the opposite of fun. Honestly, downtime may be most important item on the agenda for mom and dad, just like the kiddos. Yet, well-meaning friends may give horrible advice.

"Always schedule a date night," folks often tell young couples. Planning time to be alone seems like a good thing to do, especially as we're talking about downtime. But date nights felt pressure-packed with expectations for me. David and I like to encourage young couples by sharing how frustrating date nights were for us. As soon as we were alone, it seemed we ended up fighting. In our case, the conversation inevitably drifted to parenting issues. Disagreeing or fretting over parenting was never fun. Finally, we gave up planning date nights.

Instead, we coined one of our family mottos: "Raising children is one of the most romantic things a couple can do together." For David and me, the stilted conversations over dinner gave way to running errands together, catching a movie out, or booking a weekend away.

Being more spontaneous and free without planning made all the difference for me. I encourage you to spell out your own fun in a way that enhances freedom in your relationship. Unlike us, don't let other folks' definition of time together spell trouble for you.

Fun for couples boils down to knowing what will delight the other person. For instance, my dad romanced my mom with wacky surprises. Like the time when she was pregnant with me. They were scraping by to pay for medical school. For her birthday, he took her out for pizza, a rare treat.

Parked outside their favorite pizza joint, Mom beheld the front store window of the fancy maternity shop. Anyone who knew my cute little mom knew she never bought a new dress, always shopping thrift stores instead. Draped across the mannequin in the window like a pregnant Miss America was a pageant-style ribbon that read, "Happy Birthday, Ann." Oh, the family stories my dad created with his imaginative, fun way of romancing Mom! Fun takes on a life of its own as family legends pass through the generations.

The Sacrificial Nature of Creating Fun

Family fun evolves into family lore, passing on family values to the next generation. Families suffer because we forget fun is spiritual. Creating fun for others is a sacrificial, joy-expressing gift.

As an example, my niece collected stories as a homework assignment, which she titled "Best Christmas Ever." She asked each person in our family to tell about their favorite Christmas memory. My siblings and I all reported Meme's first airplane Christmas as our standout memory. Sorrow and sacrifice add a poignant element to that story. Because my niece took the time to capture our stories, all the next generation knows that recreation and thoughtfulness can add comfort when families grieve.

If no one helps you create fun at your house, you may have to do all the work by yourself. For a while at least. Yep, even fun requires hard work from somebody! But, you're awesome, so it's okay.

Fortunately, several things will probably happen along the way. When you create recreation for your loved ones, you might find yourself experiencing pure joy in the process. Then, when you get worn out, you can learn to enlist your husband's help.

Maybe, unlike me, you figured it out early in your marriage and asked for what you need to pull off fun family moments. I hope so! As all the happy memories start to stack up, we develop a habit of rejoicing together as a couple.

Finally, somewhere along the way your hubby will probably catch the fun bug. That's when we need to go along with his plan and encourage him in his success, even if it's a little bit of a flop at first. Next thing we know, he may be creating fun for everyone else.

Communication can be tricky in creating fun. Too much talk can ruin the spontaneity. Still, with a little conversation, creating fun for others often becomes something couples love to do together. Life is funny that way: we tend to keep what we give away.

Fun and Family Values

Fun creates lasting togetherness for all those we love, and it remains long after we are gone. Like my dad's natural knack for thoughtful surprises, fun ensures family values—such as thoughtfulness, compassion, creativity—are passed on to future generations. Fun preserves what is sacred in treasured memories and stories.

As Dad came to the close of his life, we could all tell his body was winding down. Yet, my mom insisted the last moments of their life together would not be wasted on death. She devotedly sat by and watched TV with him—a big sacrifice for a bibliophile like my mom. He slept hours of the day away because he had so little energy, yet she sat with him in quiet fellowship, book in her lap. Together, they made a daily outing for lunch. Grandchildren visited, laughing at my dad's witty comments.

Always so entertaining and funny, Dad delighted all of us who loved him right up until his breathing became so labored he could barely talk. Yet he would pull off the oxygen mask to tell us he loved us. He called us by name. We could see Mom savoring the moments. "Living in the now"[27] became one of their favorite phrases together.

Like my parents' relationship, fun cements all our relationships through shared positive experiences. It's important to share positive experiences because inevitably challenges and crises happen. How much better prepared we are to handle hardship when we've learned to create fun along the way! Besides, fun helps us cherish the moment, even when struggles seem to surround us.

Sometime after his own dad died, Dad wrote his personal obituary. Amusing our family with his practical attitude, he went ahead and wrote Mom's obituary, too. Mom and Dad accomplished a lot of worldly success in this life. However, he didn't think to include the things we loved most about him. Why would he include things that came so naturally to him?

Dad didn't think of his ability to make life fun as anything special.

27 Eckhart Tolle, *A New Earth: Awakening to Your Life's Purpose* (New York: PLUME, Penguin Group, 2005).

By writing their obituaries, he took care of us again in his far-sighted but quirky way. It's crazy what comforts you when you know your dad is dying. Knowing he captured his accomplishments on paper for us to find in his files gave us kids tender relief.

Dad was always like that—protecting us and trying to give us a life that was cushioned from the real, unavoidable suffering we all experience. Together we learned to relax in the moment and cherish each other. In the end, we edited Dad's obituary slightly to include fun. At his funeral, folks shared story after story of hilarious and tender moments with my dad.

In my mind, I am rehearsing my own obituary because it's a small thing when life still seems endless. It only takes a minute to jot down a few thoughts about life. A small thing. But now I know that, in the end, the small thoughtful things, like fun memories, become important. Fun is an essential tool to create unity in all our relationships. Especially in marriage, fun communicates worth, but it can take sacrifice. Please don't undervalue fun in your marriage. Fun secures the sacred.

In Case You Were Wondering...

I want to play with my husband, but what if he doesn't want to? If he's a young father, he's probably exhausted. Actually, old fellas get exhausted, too. Plus, he may be an introvert, defining fun as a moment of peace, not interaction. Possibly, you may be gifted at playing and he's not. Maybe his family emphasized tasks as fun, so he doesn't understand how to goof off. Or maybe all the above.

I am glad you love him because that will allow you to have compassion on him. Perhaps you can introduce a strategy for fun, like a month of fun moments broken up by the week. Week 1, fun is your responsibility. Week 2, he gets to plan a fun moment. Week 3, together you plan a fun moment for that week. Week 4, you both plan to do your own fun thing independently. Then when the month rolls over, you will enjoy doing something fun together even more because you did something separately the week before.

I encourage you to study up on being your husband's most fun friend. What do his favorite friends offer? How can those gifts translate into fun for the whole family?

If your hubby resists time off, you should take care of yourself anyway by taking breaks. One of my favorite trips without David was to Paris with our daughters and a niece. My husband was happy to let me drag anyone else into all the museums and chapels. Times apart to refresh can make coming back together even more fun and relaxed.

Pause, Ponder, Pray, and then Proceed

With fun, we preserve the sacred, especially in marriage, by encouraging fellowship and laughter. However, fun often requires more sacrifice than we may realize. Committing to fun may mean some work. Generations to come will thank you for the fun you create.

1. Understanding your needs: What is fun for each of you? What do you enjoy doing together? Once you have talked a bit about fun, schedule a little down time and give yourself permission to relax and try something new.

2. Identifying your worth: What parts of your personality come out only when you are playing? If you were to write your obituary right now, what would you write? I know it sounds morbid, but I just want you to know how loved you are long before anyone reads your obit.

3. Envisioning your future: What burden is keeping you weighed down and unable to relax? If you could do one fabulously fun thing in the near future, what would you plan and why? Who would you invite to share your fabulous fun thing? Call that person and tell them what you think is wonderful about them. Invite them to think about fun with you.

My prayer for you, with my love

Dear God, sometimes, we all feel anxious and uninspired. Help my sister think creatively about how she can bless others with the gift of fun. Let today bring a special little unexpected fun. As each little surprise unfolds, let her be aware of You, the One who gives us the best gift, Your presence. We praise You together because You are lovely to consider. Your love fills us with joy.

Together we declare with the psalmist, "But I have trusted in Your mercy; My heart shall rejoice in Your salvation. I will sing to the LORD, Because He has dealt bountifully with me" (Psalm 13:5–6).

To pray for yourself

Good Father, how can I create fun for others when I am so weighed down? I praise You because You are never worn out from hearing all my complaining and whining. You carry my load. Give me the discipline and the integrity to release myself to have some fun.

Empower me when I am uninspired. Let me experience spontaneous laughter and fun with my husband. I want to belly laugh. I want to laugh till I cry with those I love. Help me to remember what it was like to giggle like a little girl. And, dear Lord, some creative new ideas wouldn't hurt. Bless me now because that's Your heart's desire. In Jesus' name I pray. Amen.

"Fun is good." — **Dr. Seuss**

CHAPTER EIGHT

Initiating Love

Why is initiating love a sign of integrity and good leadership?
Because God loved us first.

D riving along, I was secretly savoring the last few moments as taxi mom. In a few short months, my son and all his buddies would be driving. No more candid conversations in the car. Don't all moms savor the way kids seem to talk more openly from the back seat for some reason?

"No one ever initiates," a friend piped up. Oh, my goodness, even this handsome young man with the winning personality and big heart faced the same problem all kids face along the way. Nobody initiates. Does anyone know how to reach out with a hand of friendship and loving acceptance anymore?

He raised a valid point. It seems people who initiate in relationships are few and far between. In his case, he meant no one seems to initiate friendships at school. Reaching out in school can be as simple as inviting a new student to sit next to you or offering a greeting in the hall on the way to class. Doubtlessly, what we miss as young people continues to haunt our adult relationships.

Our family, too, noticed people failed to initiate along the way. It seemed we initiated more than our fair share in all our friendships. Maybe, being an extrovert, I just needed more play dates than my friends to stay sane when the kids were little. I chalked up the missed opportunities to my own social awkwardness. Maybe I wasn't getting the social signals other people take for granted. Maybe families were just busy.

Or, maybe we were too conservative in our parenting approach. Perhaps too liberal? Who knew? As I drove the boys to our next destination, I felt comforted. Maybe it's not because my kids have a dorky mother, I thought with relief.

Young people who challenge me to think always thrill me. Trying to pass on wisdom to such smart teenagers prompted me to think a lot harder. His insight was exceptional at any age, along with his ability to articulate his thoughts. But, oh my, the question hidden in his statement inquired, "Why don't people initiate with me more?" I have often wondered why people don't like me enough to call me for coffee. Why does it seem like me doing all the reaching out?

"If people understood how God initiates and why it's so important, they would do more of it. But they don't, so it's up to you," I told him, "that's what makes you a leader." I held my breath and sighed with relief as he seemed to ponder my words. Like so many young leaders, he already noticed he was making the first move in many of his friendships. I truly admire people who can figure stuff out at a young age because youth was a serious affliction in my case.

Initiating Love: A Powerful Force for Good

As a family, we can count on one hand the people who initiated with our kids when they were growing up. Those moments stand out like sunshine after a long, dark winter. For instance, David came home one day and told me a mom called him at work to get my number.

"She heard we were living nearby out here in the country, and she heard our girls would probably like each other. She wants to get them together."

"Dave, do you realize she's initiating?" I couldn't believe it. I did all the initiating with other moms when our girls got together with friends. Plus, in our marriage, I felt like I carried the load. "We will definitely call her back," I said, overjoyed at the privilege of responding this time.

All these years later, our daughters are still the best of friends. Plus, the parents became dear friends to us, as well. Our families enjoy rich fellowship now based on years of give-and-take. All thanks to one mom's initiating love.

Offering friendship and initiating a loving relationship blesses everyone involved. It is a clear way to cherish other people, especially in marriage. Initiating sounds like a beginning, and it is. But in long-term relationships, like marriage, the beautiful process continues daily. Initiating love is a powerful force for good. Why? Because God designed us to respond to initiating love. We are like homing pigeons. He turns us loose, tossing us up to catch a gentle breeze and soar, but all the while His heart yearns for us to return to Him. In a thousand daily ways, He initiates opportunities for us to draw closely to Him. Like homing pigeons, we instinctively seek Him out, sometimes without realizing what drives us.

We belong to Him. He seeks us, too. First. Because He desires a relationship with each of us. Therefore, He initiates with us. Naturally, our hearts tingle with anticipation somewhere in a deep spiritual level when anyone initiates a relationship with us. We are hardwired to respond.

In fact, I feel so strongly about this principle I warned my girls to be careful about men who might initiate for selfish reasons. Wounded people often end up hurting others because they stumble onto one of God's laws of the universe and misuse it for their own momentary self-satisfaction. God's initiating love can be corrupted to manipulate others.

Initiating Love and Faithful, Influential Leadership

To initiate wholesome productive relationships is the mark of a humble leader. To have the kind of integrity required to initiate, we have to drill deep into our own hearts. We all want to have a husband who displays strong leadership. But as wives, we often must demonstrate strong leadership by using our influence in initiating love. Ignoring the risk of rejection, we put others ahead of ourselves, initiating again and again. When we look back in life, leaders stand out who proved to be trustworthy over the years. Often, we see the pattern of initiating, faithful friendship.

A leader's integrity stands firm in the face of life's pressures because of their humility. They foster fellowship in all their relationships in various ways. For instance, a true leader will initiate by opening the door to forgiveness and mercy when relationships get messy. Or they may initiate quiet moments together for fun. In fact, they keep initiating in all their relationships. Their respect for themselves and others empowers them to take a risk and initiate in close relationships.

Leaders who take risks by initiating demonstrate who they are and why God put them on this earth. In fact, true leaders display humility because they do not try to be self-sufficient. When pressed with many relationship demands, they will focus in on their closest relationships. All the while, they look for giftedness in others and marvel at God's provision. Not a bad way to run a business or to create a marriage and a home.

If we want to experience true oneness, we have to bravely step up and initiate. A crisis in our marriages or lives can force us to choose to be lonely or to initiate. True leaders learn to initiate no matter the crisis, especially in marriage.

In a clear illustration of the power of initiating, Michael J. Russer describes himself as the least likely person to teach about extraordinary intimacy. Yet, he shares how impotence required him to create a vision beyond the physical to the emotional and ultimately spiritual well-being of his spouse.[28] I love the definition of intimacy he developed: "I'm going to define intimacy as the deep abiding connection that can happen between two people on the emotional, physical, and even spiritual level."

A diagnosis of prostate cancer immediately after his divorce forced him to take exceptional steps to create intimacy when he met the woman he would later claim as his wife. Through their courtship, Russer learned to trust his worthiness and his ability to creatively initiate on all levels with his new love.

---

28 "Creating extraordinary intimacy in a shutdown world," Michael J. Russer, TEDx University of Nevada, https://www.youtube.com/watch?v=XK8f8w7ICng, accessed 03-24-2017.

In marriage, we face all kinds of set-backs. Changing libidos are just one of many challenges life throws at us. Can we push through the physical changes our bodies naturally go through to connect emotionally and spiritually? Of course. But it takes initiating some authentic conversations.

Initiating Toward Wisdom

Whatever challenges life dishes out, God still intends for us to express our respect for others by honoring their value and worthiness. Initiating in relationships is a great way to communicate worth. Additionally, bravely initiating new relationships and risking rejection may mean we find new friends who respond with joy and enthusiasm to our overtures.

As we advance in life, the aging process challenges us all. We discover the limits of our energy. We must treasure the time together while we still can. Yet, life's changes seem to thwart our efforts at every turn. Particularly in marriage, initiating conversations and trying new solutions gets old. We all get tired of trying when nothing seems to work. When David and I hit the twenty-year mark, for example, things began to unravel quickly in our marriage. So, I called my mom for some encouragement one day, complaining about how Dave blamed my bad mood on menopause.

"You know, Cathy, men go through menopause, too," she said. Since then, I've Googled "manopause" many times. Mom was way ahead of her time when it came to understanding the aging process for men, as well as women.

Suddenly, I appreciated the way God designed men to slow down. I began to respect the slow process of maturing in wisdom while aging physically. Our world certainly can use all the wise people we can get.

Rejection Short-circuits Leadership

In particular, one aspect of wisdom, responding lovingly in the face of rejection, challenges us when it comes to initiating. Why don't folks initiate? By folks, let's face it, I really mean our husbands. Why don't our husbands initiate gentle conversations or romantic fun or other expressions of their affection?

People don't initiate because other people tend to reject. We are so used to rejection, we assume other people will reject, even when they don't. In fact, a gruff edge in a spouse's voice may seem like rejection, even if unintentional. Naturally, we all get discouraged in the face of impatience, for instance. With rejection—real or imagined—initiating becomes more difficult for both people. This is especially true for a husband and wife.

First, it becomes more difficult for the person who initiated and felt rejected. We tend to keep score of rejection subconsciously and get skittish. Second, though, it becomes surprisingly harder for the rejecter to initiate in the future. Why? Because that person knows somewhere deep down that rejection is likely, since he practices it himself. He may even feel like he deserves to be rejected.

For example, let's say a husband chooses to respond gruffly or impatiently, rather than gently, when you initiate. I'm not talking sex here. Seriously, is it just me or do men seem to struggle with a disconnect when it comes to kindness and sex? There are shelves of books written on the male and female physiological differences. It seems all couples struggle to communicate clearly about when a spouse is offering kindness or when a spouse is initiating a sexual encounter. Sex and kindness are closely related.

However, in this case, I'm talking about offering simple kindness. Maybe his back hurts or he is worried about work, so he acts grumpy or impatient in response to your kind offer. Even a momentary self-indulgence, choosing to respond gruffly, conveys a huge cache of rejection.

By rejecting you with impatience or grumpiness, he makes himself more vulnerable to self-rejection. As the days go by, it becomes easier for him to imagine you holding him in contempt, shame, unworthiness, etc. Because he knows he was unkind in the face of your kindness, he will find it easier to imagine your frustration and unforgiveness. A simple apology would fix the discomfort, but we tend to let small things go without talking about them.

Negative emotions—even imagined ones—are poison to unity. Unless we have the courage to talk them out, our self-indulgent habits will permeate and destroy the relationship. Rejection is messy business. It's rooted in low self-worth, by the way.

Initiating and Integrity

Initiating new habits is a sign of integrity. Good communication habits develop around a commitment to talk about any real or imagined sense of rejection. Simple questions like, "What's going on with you? Anything I can do to comfort or encourage?" may shed light on the real situation and release both spouses from imagining foolish scenarios.

The fact that my young friend could not understand why people fail to initiate tells me his parents have done an excellent job of modeling unfailing, initiating love for him. Oh, if only more young men were trained in those qualities! We want our children to have the ability to initiate loving relationships and keep initiating unfailing kindness. Even if we learn together as we go, we can give this gift to our children.

How do we know initiating love is a sign of integrity and true leadership? God initiates. He demonstrates His initiating love toward us in His Son's life on Earth as recorded in the New Testament book of John by eyewitnesses. There we read about how God sought us out to know Him (John 3:16).

The man or woman who desires to initiate love in the face of rejection has a great example in Jesus' life and words. We can make God's character known in our marriages by initiating love, even when it feels like we are facing rejection. We could even define grace as the ongoing process of initiating love.

Grace, Not Codependence

Please do not confuse initiating love with codependence. Marriage can be a painful process. Even though I am not a marriage therapist, your safety should be an obvious concern for anyone who loves you.

If you feel threatened in any way, please seek good advice from people who are trained in counseling. When you initiate loving interactions, please simultaneously take the steps necessary to always keep yourself physically, emotionally, and spiritually healthy. Always establish appropriate boundaries.

The way God keeps initiating a loving relationship in the face of our ongoing rejection is a perfect example of His grace. He initiated a way for us to know Him. His disciples recorded His message for us. Miraculously, God preserved the Bible, one of the most-read, beloved volumes of all time throughout history. There we read of men and women just like us who turned away from His love. Yet, He kept the door open for anyone who responded to return to Him, even as He respected their decision to reject Him.

Like so many in the centuries before us, we mess up, we turn to Him, and He forgives us. God exercises patient, long-waiting love while we exercise our free will to ignore Him. Grace is what God gives us while He waits for us to figure out we need His mercy. Mercy is the forgiveness He offers the instant we ask for it. Mercy is already paid for by His Son. It's pretty easy to tell grace and mercy apart. Mercy happens instantly. Grace involves an extended time. Both are repetitive cycles because of our human tendency to choose selfishly. Both grace and mercy reflect God's unfailing, initiating love for us.

God initiates. We reject. God initiates again anyway. Grace is an essential element of fellowship. To better understanding God's patient, enduring love for us we must offer grace to others, too.

Looking Past Now to Eternity

When David and I were dating, I put up a big barrier at one point and intended to break off the relationship. Contrary to my plans, David showed up at a party in my parents' home. Even after all the other guests were gone, he kept hanging around. In a courageous feat of initiative, David asked me to dinner, ignoring my cool attitude. Sometimes as women, we fail to recognize how hard it can be for men to initiate. Before I could reject his offer, Meme spoke up.

"Cathy is free tonight. She would love to go to dinner with you."

Thanks to Meme, David and I went to dinner that night. Surprisingly, the relationship took an unexpected turn. David was looking past the momentary now to a future I couldn't see yet. Looking past the now into eternity gives us more patience and energy to be faithful in the face of minor, momentary rejections.

Sometimes God just initiates love with us until we finally run out of excuses. God's integrity and autonomy are demonstrated in the way He is free to initiate a loving relationship. He does not fold in the face of our anticipated rejection. He knows what He wants. God wants companionship with us. He delights in each one of us. He is a gentle and respectful Friend, only wanting what is healthy and best for each of His children.

I actually ask David pretty regularly if he loves me. I'm that insecure. Or I ask another favorite question, *Why do you love me?* That's a fun question because he tries to answer it for me. I know not every woman is blessed with such a patient husband. It took David years to realize I wasn't kidding about feeling insecure. My bold personality confused him. He honestly didn't know how fearful I can feel. I had to get real with him and be vulnerable about where I felt unworthy.

Living With the Rejection of an Unspiritual Man

I realize some women suffer because they are married to men who do not know Jesus—yet. Remember Jesus came to seek and save the lost. He desires us to put aside conflict with those who don't know His beloved Son and invite them into a friendship with Him.

Many women suffer because they feel their husband does not love them the way a spiritual man should. *Does my husband love me?* This could be my favorite breathtakingly honest question in the whole book. This nagging insecurity is probably why women my age say they will never marry again because "it takes too long to train a husband."

Since we believe all women can move from co-existing to being cherished through great conversations, I have not forgotten the wife longing to win her husband to Christ. I have some thoughts to encourage you and offer you hope.

I truly love conversations with agnostics and atheists. I love how honest they are about their lack of faith in God. Claiming agnosticism or atheism means that person is committed to two of my all-time favorite questions! *Does God exist? If He does exist, how could we possibly know Him?* What a great place to initiate an on-going, authentic, sacred, respectful conversation!

For starters, I never argue about faith or religion. If God respects people's right to decide, shouldn't I? Instead of promoting my agenda, I find people are generous in sharing when we ask gentle questions.

I am including a few of my favorite questions below, realizing you may live with a man whose perspective on faith differs from yours. This can cause all kinds of discomfort and arguments in marriage. We need to develop skills to manage our conflicts at home, especially on the topic of religion (or lack of it).

I always begin by asking two questions. Do you believe you have a spirit? After we've talked a while, I ask another favorite question. Would the person like for me to pray for them? In my experience, most folks want prayer, no matter their religious perspectives. There's something so loving about praying to God for another human's best welfare.

By asking those two questions as a lifestyle over the years, I accidentally discovered two things. First, everyone seems to agree they have a spirit. Secondly, in all these years, I only had one person say no to prayer.

Conversation is a serious art form, requiring training and years of practice. Initiating love means we let down our walls and tell the truth about where we hurt. Such authenticity is a rare skill set indeed! People who master the art of conversation develop skill at asking the right gentle questions. They begin to see the fruit in their lives as their marriages develop fellowship. They will probably see those they love learn to understand God better. This process can take years. If you initiate such encounters with those you love starting today, you'll experience the joy of tender conversations much sooner.

Initiating Out of Confident Integrity

To initiate with confident integrity, you must value yourself. You are truly a miracle. Just the atomic substructure in your body boggles comprehension. Then there's all the DNA and experiences that came together to form the personality you now rock in your uniquely creative and breathtaking way. Plus, your whole spiritual dimension is unfathomable, mysterious, and well, incredibly sexy. What's not to love! God knows all this about you and loves you like you're the only person in the universe.

Confidence in God's initiating, unfailing love translates itself into leadership and influence. As we experience His delight in us, we find it easier to shake off the rejection of others. Our minds recognize the trap of rejection when we see it in others' behaviors. We choose freedom and wholeheartedness one small initiating act at a time. Soon, our lives and our habits follow.

When we focus on God's love for us, we focus on eternity. Instead of getting trapped in a momentary relationship mess, we are free to shake off rejection from others. Lo and behold, we are free from distraction. We find we have the energy we need to accomplish the beautiful things God intends for us to accomplish, including building rich, tender relationships with the friends and loved ones He provides.

Loving with dignity, even in the face of rejection, we freely ensure our own safety, too. Grace habitually informs us as we keep on loving and initiating. We free ourselves to delight in our marriages and all our relationships. Soon, we experience the deep fellowship our lives were designed to reflect.

In Case You Were Wondering...

How do I initiate love and leadership when my husband is supposed to be the spiritual leader? First, your husband is your spiritual leader because God set the role aside for him. But, okay, I admit—in Texas, we pioneer women strengthen our men with "git your rear in gear" moments sometimes. We even have what we call "Come to Jesus" moments, meaning we have a serious talk and expect change in behavior and attitude.

God extends the initiating leadership role to us all, male and female, by His own example. Initiating love is one of the most powerful, transformative forces in the universe. It ought to have its own place in the superpowers hall of fame. Miraculously, when we send God's love out into the universe, it tends to come home again to us, like a boomerang.

We embrace God's initiating love for us when we turn to trustworthy friends. For example, by sharing your true question, you've opened the door to my heart. We relate to others' pain because we've all experienced pain. We offer comfort because we've experienced the need for it.

Our enemy wants us to be so beat down we're of no use to God's people. Please look around for the small ways God is communicating His initiating love for you, in the small furry creature who scampers across your path, in the triumphant notes of a song at church, in an awe-inspiring sunset, in the hug of a true friend.

Additionally, may I offer you this? Even when your hubby fails to initiate loving leadership, you are lovable, especially to God. Learning to initiate loving relationships is its own miracle.

Pause, Ponder, Pray, and then Proceed

We initiate loving affection because God designed us to create a lifetime of unselfconscious affection. If you get to spend time around small cuddly toddlers, you know exactly what I mean. They are irresistible, even on their grumpiest days.

1. Understanding your needs: Who in your life faithfully sets an example of initiating leadership by consistently reaching out to friends? What thoughts or specific past rejections tend to hinder you when it comes to initiating with others? Today, please ask a trusted friend for coffee for no reason except to prove to yourself you have what it takes to be an initiating leader.

2. Identifying your worth: How can you free up some time this week

to spend with close friends? What task can you cut from your schedule this month to find a little extra energy to cherish your hubby by initiating kindness with him?

You may laugh at this, but at my house, an initiating act of love is to sit and watch television with my hubby. It's so hard for me to sit still, sometimes I have to read a chapter during the commercials.

3. Envisioning your future: Who would respond joyfully today if you initiated a moment by making a quick phone call to say hi? Tonight when you see your husband, what small kindness could you speak to initiate loving affection? For instance, the simple act of greeting each other with a big smile is a great way to initiate loving leadership in our homes.

My prayer for you, with my love

Dear God, please bless my sister, even when she feels worn out or rejection triggers a prideful response. Give her the energy she needs today to ignore distractions. At work and at home, energize her to express her respect for all and her affection for those she loves. Let her experience the delight of having people seek her out. Make her aware when others initiate with her. Open her eyes when her hubby initiates with her in ways she may not have ever recognized before. Help her respond with joy and delight.

Together we claim this beautiful promise excerpted from the Psalms, "He who walks uprightly, And works righteousness, And speaks the truth in his heart...He who does these *things* shall never be moved" (Psalm 15:2, 5).

To pray for yourself

Good Father, You are the One who leads me in Your everlasting ways. Your ways are higher and richer than I know. I am Yours. My pleasure is to follow You. You initiate with me constantly, and my heart responds with joy when I notice. Help me notice. When I feel worn out, show me the resources and strength I have in You. Give me victorious truth today over any self-rejecting thoughts. When my pride and insecurity torment me, help me feel secure in Your love and leadership. Give my family the grace of Your initiating love. Lead my husband now and in the future. I will gladly shout Your praises because You are mighty. I praise You, O Holy One. Bless me now because that's Your heart's desire. In Jesus' name. Amen.

"Leadership is influence." — **John C. Maxwell**

Part Two
The How-Tos of Marriage

CHAPTER NINE

Continental Divide

**Why do we have to learn everything
the hard way and be divided?**
*Because we are human, we forget
to humbly seek truth.*

Oturning point came in our marriage on the way to Branson to celebrate my parents' fiftieth wedding anniversary. Just planning the trip challenged us all. With extended family members tackling detailed arrangements and voicing opinions, we needed a rest before we packed up! We needed fun, within driving range, plus a hospital nearby just in case, heaven forbid.

As the trip got closer, my anxiety increased. Marriage was on my mind, but not in a good way. Our own anniversary follows closely behind Mom and Dad's. I heard my martyr voice saying out loud, "I put up with this for twenty years." Sadly, as we faced the nine-hour drive, I suspected our boiling point was gaining on us. Car confinement with attitudes getting stinky: not a promising mix! And I'm talking about us, not our kids! We were only as far as Arkansas, yet David and I teetered one word away from an argument.

Then it happened. Our son, not quite thirteen, announced in a loud voice he didn't wash his hands in the bathroom of a fast-food restaurant. This was a direct challenge to my standing rule, *Always wash hands*. I instructed him to return to the bathroom and wash his hands. He threw out his chest, straightened his back like his adulthood was at stake and flat-out refused. Well, now, there's a new wrinkle, I thought, gazing up at this six-foot tall human I had given birth to only a few years prior.

I looked to David for back up. Instead, David agreed with our son and scolded me in front of our children. Really? I was livid. I marched to our van like a tin soldier on a mission. Tense silence reigned in the van for miles. Finally, in the next town, David stopped for a huge bottle of hand sanitizer. Problem solved, right?

Not hardly. I'm pretty sure there was smoke coming out my ears. Disproportionate anger tormented me. Such a little thing, such red-hot anger. I can't explain the rage I felt, except to say I let one too many boundaries go. After another half hour of deathly silence, I finally put words to my dilemma.

"You owe me an apology for not backing me up about the hand washing. I want it in front of the kids because you were disrespectful of me in front of them. You can make any decision you want to, but that's what I want to happen." I was staking out some new ground in our marriage. If respect was good for the gander, the goose wanted it, too.

Uncomfortable Silence

David explained how I was not thinking rationally about it. For the next several miles, he reasoned with me. Obviously, hand sanitizer beats hand-washing in dirty public bathrooms. I was making a scene by insisting out loud in a packed restaurant when our son refused to obey. This was a conversation (read argument) we should have in private. Etc. Etc. Etc. Looking back, I'm pretty sure I was totally irrational in that moment.

His reasoning washed over me like so much nonsense. Finally, I saw the situation for what it was. We had double standards. For the next few miles, I reminded him of his rules: always back me up, never correct me in front of the kids, disagree in private later. The only new boundary was no double standards. As mile stretched into mile, my anger faded, and icy emotional temperatures replaced hot tempers in the car.

We traveled in uncomfortable silence to celebrate my parents' fiftieth. Ironically, I would be lucky if we made our twenty-fifth. Oneness was the last thing on my mind. Honestly, my thoughts went like this as I began to calm down: *How did I get to this spot? How do I get out of it?*

Imagine the relief our children felt when their dad finally apologized to me—in front of them and God and probably a host of astonished angels, glory hallelujah! What a gift of humility he decided to give me that day! Even though I know America's continental divide is in the Rockies, I always think of our marital continental divide as somewhere right outside of Branson, Missouri, just in the nick of time.

The Continental Divide of What Works in Marriage

I reached another continental divide that day, a new way of thinking. Instead of focusing on the whys of marriage, I began to search for the hows. Sure, I understood the why of our conflict, "Why did we have a double standard?" But I discovered the how was more important to me, "How do I make a small change here without swamping our marriage?"

In this book, we've reached a continental divide. The first section was about the whys of marriage. Now we're going to focus on the how-tos. We are seeking truth about how good communications skills can create a unified, harmonious marriage and life.

For instance, to David, my focus on hand washing seemed irrational. He never would have thought to apologize except I asked for it. After twenty years of marriage, I was learning an important truth. I needed healthy boundaries. In order to create healthy boundaries, I had to know what I wanted. Could I learn to ask for what I wanted? To do so, I had to believe God wanted good things for me.

Once I knew what I wanted—the good, wholesome things God wants for all of us—I could speak clearly to my desire. That could change every conversation afterwards. For instance, I could put my foot down about double standards. If only I could figure out where the double standards existed in our marriage.

My dad used to say, "Cathy, why do you always have to learn everything the hard way?" Most of my life, I thought everyone learned by trial and error. In my case, lots of error. *There's an easy way? Someone should have told me before my life got so messed up.*

I Had a Lot to Learn

I learned much later in life many of the struggles we all face are unnecessary. For instance, you don't have to make the same mistakes I made. As humbly as I know how, I've shared many of my mistakes in these stories. Together, we can search out good ideas and save ourselves lots of heartache in the future.

When it comes to communicating in our marriage, I was a slow learner again. I loved our marriage and worked hard to keep it afloat. In spite of extensive training and experience in communications, I had a lot to learn when it came to having authentic marriage conversations. You know the kind I mean. Not the ones that devolve into arguments. No sir. I wanted tender conversations, leading to increased intimacy, understanding, and joy.

We'll discuss a host of practical communication principles. We're going to look at family mission statements, how hospitality transforms our own hearts, even how to negotiate like an oil tycoon. Why do these ideas matter? Because seeking truth together unites us, even if the way seems rocky at times. In marriage, the choice between division or unity becomes a fundamental issue. Unity is often only one conversation away.

People end up divided because they fail to seek truth. In marriage, divisions creep up insidiously, like termites eating away silently behind walls. Conversely, truth sets us free. To achieve freedom nearly always means developing a habit of humbleness. The work of freedom and unity includes creating authentic conversations with vulnerability and patience. Then, freedom unites us.

The idea of freedom uniting us sounds kinda crazy when you consider America's rollicking political discussions with all the opinionated, controversial ideologues. Oh, the polarization! Part of the problem in American politics is definitely pride.

Learning to cherish each other is as simple as learning some basic communication how-tos. However, when freedom and truth are united with humility, heavenly harmony breaks out, almost like a song of joy. Freedom and humility are the only way to be united, especially in marriage.

Moving forward freely

Freedom comes to us when we humbly seek truth. Even if your husband fails to seek truth, you can begin to build freedom and joy into your relationship. God offers wisdom; we seek it. With wisdom, we receive freedom and joy. What woman doesn't love a great bonus deal like that!

Once I began to conscientiously and humbly collect lots of good ideas from experts, my heart wanted to get their ideas on record. I began to write, first, for my own kiddos, then for you. Thank you for reading through the philosophical stuff to this point.

Like the turning point near Branson in my marriage, now we'll turn to the practical stuff. We'll ask the how question I asked outside of Branson, *How do we move forward?* We'll look at some basic communication strategies and how they can transform your marriage and family communication.

Personally, I love the big why questions, the fundamental, foundational, philosophical truths. Good stuff. I hope, like me, your brain and heart get excited contemplating the big why questions of life. However, sometimes we need to get nitty-gritty and just get the job done. When it comes to great marriage conversations, the how-tos are what make today a little better and tomorrow a little brighter.

We'll cover stuff like how to get through to your husband when his baggage short-circuits his listening ability. Plus, if you are like me and you need fresh ideas on how to create a unifying vision for your marriage, please keep reading.

Even before I married David, I started making note of the happy couples around me that seemed to have it. The *it* turned out to be fellowship. Their harmony was based on their ability to have authentic conversations.

Then, later, our young son put together a neighborhood newspaper for several years, interviewing all couples who reached the fifty-year mark. We unraveled secrets to good marriages as they shared their stories and advice each week.

All along the way, with each bump in the road, Dave and I sought out professional advice from a trusted counselor. We spent more than our fair share of time on his couch. Paying someone else was far easier than learning the hard way.

The How-tos of Marriage Conversation

Almost forty years later, I'm now convinced the nuts and bolts of good marriages are in the how questions. I'm excited about the following chapters. When it comes to cherishing each other, it turns out success is in the how-tos of great conversations.

If you are looking for Dr. Lexicon, the guy with the big vocabulary and glamorous credentials, you've come to the wrong place. If you are looking to debate the issues, I am sorry to report that I reached my argument quota a long time ago deciding important issues like whether to use the sink or hand sanitizer.

On the other hand, if you're looking for someone who knows how to be real, who respects your privilege to think for yourself, and who does not mind sharing her secrets (yes, even her mistakes), you've come to the right place. Foundational truths, the whys of marriage, transformed our journey as we began. But from this point, we explore the practical skills to make authentic conversations an integral part of our marriage. In marriage, we enjoy the rare privilege of humbly seeking truth together. What joy! If you want a friend who won't judge, then keep reading as we cross the continental divide together.

In Case You Were Wondering...

I want to speak up, but what if I am afraid of division in our marriage? That's a legitimate concern. In my own marriage, speaking up often highlights concerns we wanted to ignore. Ouch! Open conflict can follow.

One option is to keep pretending the problem isn't real. Should we "go along to get along," as some might suggest? Or "shut up and put up"? I like the idea of pausing, praying, pondering, and then proceeding with a good strategy to have the necessary marriage conversations.

Certainly, the habit of going along to avoid drama tempts us all. If we're honest, even the feistiest prefer to avoid conflict. But our silence creates an unnatural divide.

Division is the opposite of oneness. We must speak up. Courage and truthfulness are required. With so many attacks on openness, you might think an enemy conspires to silence us. The Bible gives us a hint of whom we're facing, "Be sober, be vigilant; because your adversary the devil walks about like a roaring lion, seeking whom he may devour" (1 Peter 5:8).

Knowing we actually have a real enemy means we absolutely need to speak up. Seeking truth together requires us to humbly focus on the how-tos of great relationships. We all crave authentic conversations. We want to cherish each other. It may seem like climbing a mountain to get there, but great conversations mean many happy roads ahead for your marriage and your family.

Pause, Ponder, Pray, and then Proceed

We are often slow to apply the truths we need. Sometimes, the continental divide in a relationship becomes the place where two people go different ways. Instead, let's go to God, the One who formed continents, to teach us how to be united in our marriage.

1. Understanding your needs: You probably already have some crucial communication skills you use daily, maybe without even knowing how well you handle certain situations. What skills do you already use to help you eliminate any division in your marriage? What new skills could be valuable assets for you?

To start a new kind of conversation at dinner tonight, plan ahead with a humble question, like "What new thing did you learn today?" or "If you could change one thing in the world, what would it be?"

2. Identifying your worth: What kind of gentle patience are you willing to extend to your husband, knowing you deserve the same kind-

ness? What moments in your life have been continental divides, the big turning points? Share your big moment with a trustworthy friend or your grown children. Those personal stories are priceless.

3. Envisioning your future: As the Lord shows you how to be more unified with your husband, what areas could use some small changes today? If God wanted to give your kids a gift of something heavenly and harmonious, what would you ask Him for on their behalf? Sometimes, heavenly harmony is exactly what God wants to give our kids.

My prayer for you, with my love

Dear God, we travel through life surrounded by people who count on us to be our best on their behalf. We all have moments when confusion and division seem to prevail in our marriages. Yet, You have chosen this sister to make a significant impact for Your kingdom. You intend for her to honor You in her marriage. She will need Your help. Thank You for being a God who does not tolerate double standards but gently corrects them. Teach her to learn the easy way.

Together we rejoice from Psalm 16, "I will bless the LORD who has given me counsel; My heart also instructs me in the night seasons. I have set the LORD always before me; Because *He is* at my right hand I shall not be moved. Therefore my heart is glad, and my glory rejoices; My flesh also will rest in hope" (verses 7–9).

To pray for yourself

Good Father, You are the One who sends Your gentle Helper, Your Holy Spirit. Because of You, I am well-coached and ready for action. When I feel confused, give me clarity and let me know Your counsel. When my marriage feels divided, give me the vision to see past the divide to Your presence. Give me patience. Let us rejoice in our marriage. Teach me to be a faithful guide to others who choose the road of Your wonderful kingdom. I praise You, O Lord, Ruler of all. Bless me now because that's Your heart's desire. In Jesus' name I pray. Amen.

"Do not long for others to look upon you and say, 'That person is wise.' Rather, hope for this awe-filled whisper: 'They are a blessing.'" —**Benjamin A. Simpson,** Writer

CHAPTER TEN

Queen of the Dirty Laundry

How does creating a personal etiquette free us up?
By teaching us to know ourselves.

D amn cat," I said to Mom, paying close attention to gauge her reaction. There was something tricky about my new vocabulary word. Not quite sure what would happen next, with a clear conscious, my four-year-old heart anticipated a reaction.

"Never let me hear you use that word," she replied with ominous calm.

"Why not? Dad says 'damn cat.'"

Apparently, there are many good reasons not to use that word. Perhaps she numbered them with the flat of her hand applied not-so-gently to my hindquarter. If so, my mind has forever rendered that part of the episode to regions inaccessible. Most likely, she enumerated the reasons with a steady, determined voice until my will finally, inevitably crumbled before the strength of hers. That was more her style—Mom came from Texas pioneer stock.

The next thing I remember about the "*damn* incident" was sprawling myself out on a pile of dirty laundry. A self-righteous stew settled over me as I contemplated injustice in the hallway of the little bungalow my parents owned in Galveston.

Their first adventure in home ownership, the tiny dream house sported xeriscaping long before it trended. My baby sister and I shared a room fitted with twin beds perfectly balanced on either side of a big window. Down the hall was the baby-sized extra room that soon morphed into my brother's nursery. With a linen-stuffed closet, our cat spotted the perfect birthing room for a litter of kittens. What a mess!

"Daddy says that word all the time," I mumbled loudly into a pile of his dirty T-shirts, smelling comfortingly of him. "Just wait until he gets home and I tell him what Mom said."

"Humph," said my mom to no one in particular as she walked by, loaded down with the first basket of clean, neatly folded clothes.

From my vantage point as queen of the dirty laundry, I pondered the obvious hypocrisy that happens in families. Oh, the injustice of life!

Later in the evening, when my dad finally got home from working a twelve-hour shift at the hospital, he briefly confirmed he indeed forbade me from repeating every cotton-picking word he said. I'm convinced the discussion continued long after their young daughters drifted off to sleep. But apparently whatever they said to each other never interfered with producing my baby brother.

Committed to Her Values

My mom's steady commitment to be true to her values meant her kids often got to observe two ways of doing things. Her values included good manners and proper etiquette. Perhaps because my dad grew up in a formal home, he indulged in a more casual attitude. They represented two different perspectives, two sets of boundaries and, in many ways, two sets of values. Yet, I often witnessed how my mother's personal etiquette freed her to communicate gently with my dad.

Somehow my mom managed to stay true to herself. As we say in Texas, "She stuck to her guns!" Her personal etiquette never depended on a set of rules or making others live by her values. Instead, my earliest childhood memories include how Mom's personal etiquette shaped the tender habits of our home life. Without making a big fuss about it most of the time, she quietly put down boundaries, even with my dad. Her personal etiquette included knowing herself well. She knew what she stood for and she lived it out, sometimes in the face of opposition.

Because of Mom's fortitude, I experienced firsthand how limits can powerfully influence a husband's perspective. Her quiet, personal etiquette molded our young hearts and established respect in our home. Honestly, like doing loads of laundry, when it comes to boundaries, circumstances may require us to follow her example and simply do the dirty work ourselves.

Living by our standards in the face of opposition is actually a blessing, as difficult as it may seem at first glance. Why? Because knowing our personal etiquette helps us know ourselves. What a lovely reward!

Boundaries at Home

In order to figure out what our limits look like, we can ask two simple questions: What am I willing to put up with? What crosses the line? Ultimately, the answers to those two questions form our personal etiquette or boundaries. In fact, defining your own limits, allows you to discover what issues trigger your own conscience. Consequently, your conscience defines your choices and lifestyle. Then, significantly, your lifestyle informs your children.

Once our boundaries settle into place consistently, we freely give out the same respectful treatment we expect from others. Respect cuts both ways in all our relationships. The Golden Rule takes on life in our hearts as we treat others the way we expect to be treated. Maybe it seems trite to the rest of the world, but for me, the Golden Rule inspires joy in my heart. Perhaps only a girl who discovered the Bible later in life rejoices at the miraculous mystery of Jesus' wisdom in this one simple sentence: "Do unto others as you would have them do unto you."

Therefore, establishing a personal etiquette for ourselves provides a secure foundation for our own consciences. Families can then establish patterns and habits to define respectful manners at home. When we know what our personal etiquette is, we soon discover the good manners we want to extend to others. Good manners, cherishing each other, and our own personal etiquette go hand in hand.

Soon, good manners become our lifestyle because we know what our own personal etiquette requires of us. In other words, we're seeking a lifestyle that reflects a clear conscience. I wonder why good manners are so underrated in the culture we live in today.

Good manners and personal etiquette are a way of spreading kindness. Etiquette clarifies boundaries for everyone in your home, your church, your community. Good manners form the quickest short cut to trust. Harmony, enhanced by good manners, can set the tone for all our relationships, especially in marriage. Your own personal etiquette defines how you treat people even when they behave unkindly or rudely. Thus, personal etiquette begins to shape your integrity; that is, who you are.

It is not my job to make my husband abide by my personal etiquette. I don't try to control him. I can trust the Savior who died for us both to guide my husband, even when I disagree with his decisions.

Likewise, I am free to make the decisions my conscience requires of me. My personal etiquette helps me stick to my convictions, even when David disagrees with me. We don't have to reject each other simply because we disagree. We are free to disagree and still enjoy each other.

My mom was a terrific example of sticking to her principles while still enjoying my dad's hilarious antics. Still, all married couples have moments when their conscience may require one of them to say no. Mom was no exception. I clearly remember difficult times when she simply said no.

No! Not Just for Toddlers

In our family we always laugh when one of the toddlers begins to experiment with the word, "No!" It's a useful word for all humans to wield with force. I was thrilled to let my daughters learn the power of *no* early in their lives, probably because I had so many mishaps as a wild teenager when I caved into peer pressure.

Because my mom respected herself, she said no often. My dad's alcohol consumption offers a case in point. When I was growing up, Alcoholics Anonymous was not a common thing. Back then, if someone was lying in the gutter, they wore the label *drunk*. The culture designated everyone else who habitually drank as "social drinkers."

Long before society recognized drinking and driving as an issue and a felony, my mom always took the keys away from Dad. She drove us home. This was not a personality trait on her part. Instead, it cost her to stand up to Dad.

Honestly, when I think about her courage, I don't know how it would have ended if he refused to give up the keys. Mom was a creative and determined gal. I bet she would have called a cab and taken her children home with or without Dad.

Even as I write about those years, my heart breaks for women in difficult situations today with a man they love. We simply cannot control other adults. In difficult decision moments, a personal etiquette informs us when it's time to choose between safety and a man we love. I hope you are not in a situation where you need to make such decision. But if you are, I encourage you to wisely secure safety for yourself and your children.

Mom's personal etiquette strengthened her resolve to say no when necessary. Instead of caving, she simply recognized the danger and respected herself and her kids too much to let Dad drive. Occasionally he resisted her, but Mom steadfastly clung onto the keys. Looking back, her personal etiquette defined their marriage and demonstrated resolve for the hearts of her kids.

There were moments when Dad was disrespectful, treating her like a kill joy for spoiling his alcohol-induced fun. But even in his worst moments, Mom's strength inspired Dad's respect. Later in life, after he found recovery and sobriety one day at a time, our dad would often praise our mom's fortitude.

Defined Etiquette Creates Mutual Respect

Her personal etiquette always enhanced the tenderness they enjoyed. That is not the case for everyone. Some husbands refuse to respect boundaries. I'm grateful my strong mom found the balance between saying no to my dad and enjoying him anyway. My prayer for you is if you find yourself in such a situation you find the strength to receive the blessing of safety God desires to give you, however that looks.

As women, when we fail to determine our own boundaries, we run into problems. Our love creates a desire to please a husband. In fact, without a defined personal etiquette in place, we develop bad habits. We make uncomfortable compromises and then regret our decisions. We fail to speak up when we should. We miss the life-changing opportunities provided by authentic conversations.

With undefined boundaries, couples often experience discord and disunity. Defined etiquette creates mutual respect and spells out expectations. We can have conversations with our husband about our personal etiquette, but only if we define it first. This may be a short conversation if we have to say to a husband, "No, I'm not comfortable doing that."

I can't emphasize enough that personal etiquette is not about forcing others to conform to our values. Instead, we search for truth about human relationships to form principles we respect personally. The Bible makes a fine foundation for a personal etiquette, affirming a basic truth. We each deserve to be treated respectfully, even as we treat others so.

When it comes to forming a personal etiquette, I like simple. Why? Because I find simple stuff easier to remember. Especially when I'm sorely tempted to break my own etiquette. Therefore, I want to share mine, in case you want something simple. My personal etiquette echoes in my heart, "Be kind." That's about as simple as it gets. Is it pretty pathetic that I have to remind myself to be kind? Sad, but true.

Even though I prefer easy-to-remember, I know women who keep a long list on the fridge to strengthen themselves. Maybe you've been in classrooms where formidable teachers clarify respect in posters spelling it out. Usually, the list includes broad ideas like "Use good manners," that can be applied to almost any circumstance with a question, like "Is it good manners to interrupt the conversation?" Having a personal etiquette helps us to practice patience, whether it's in the classroom or at home.

Prayers, verses, or poems can be memorized to remind us who we are and what we stand for. For instance, I like the Serenity Prayer for obvious reasons. "God, grant me the serenity to accept the things I cannot change, courage to change the things I can, and wisdom to know the difference," written by American theologian Reinhold Niebuhr in 1934,[29] the same year my parents were born.

The Bible offers countless wonderful choices for creating our own personal etiquette from the prayers, poems, proverbs, and words of encouragement written there. For one favorite example, I love "Finally, brethren, whatever things are true, whatever things *are* noble, whatever things *are* just, whatever things *are* pure, whatever things *are* lovely, whatever things *are* of good report, if there *is* any virtue and if *there is* anything praiseworthy—meditate on these things" (Philippians 4:8). This verse always serves to keep my mind in check. Usually, my manners follow closely enough to keep my conscience clear.

Another advantage to searching for biblical truth for your guidelines on good manners includes the way Scripture strengthens our core sense of our own value. As surely as spring follows winter, the more versed we become in a lifestyle based on Scripture, the more tender we become with others.

On Upright Trajectory

Blessedly, we sidestep most of everyone else's drama and trauma by respecting others. In choosing good manners, we set ourselves free to realize our own potential without distractions. While others misbehave, we forego the nastiness. Why? Because we know who we are and that's not us.

Plainly, there's another advantage to keeping the eternal in sight when defining personal etiquette. Thoughts of eternity set a life's trajectory. Fortunately, just like my mom, we can set a trajectory using personal etiquette, even if our spouses think it sounds wacky at first.

In the oil business, we understand the idea of trajectories because we have a concept called the "true inclination" when drilling an oil well. A highly technical term, the true inclination of an oil well refers to measuring the angle of the drilling pipe as you drill down into the earth. Petroleum engineers are trained to analyze the true inclination of the hole with tools designed especially for this essential function. A

---

29 Serenity Prayer, https://en.wikipedia.org/wiki/Serenity_Prayer, accessed 11-10-16

personal etiquette acts like a tool to measure whether our inclinations stay on track so our life's trajectory stays on the course we choose.

In the oil business, keeping a straight, vertical angle means crucial success. When your drill bit accesses the earth's structure in the proper formation, we all gain oil or gas to fuel our culture's electrical and transportation needs. In Texas and many other states, local communities build schools and infrastructure with the tax revenues.

Sadly, straying off course on a false trajectory can cost millions in lost tax revenue for community endeavors. Especially in the energy business, families depend on jobs provided when oil producers define true inclinations correctly. Like true inclinations, a personal etiquette provides a trustworthy trajectory for all our relationships, especially in marriage.

In the oil business like life, digging deep, straight, and true makes me think of the word *upright*. Certainly, upright describes my mom, who happened to be a geologist, by the way. *Upright* best describes the benefit of choosing a personal etiquette. When life tries to knock us down, a personal etiquette keeps us upright. Above all, knowing who we are even empowers us to stand alone when necessary.

Our children benefit in those moments when we stand alone. We can create our personal etiquette for the sake of our kids, even if we don't do it for our own sweet and worthy self. A mom's true and upright perspective on herself will fuel her children's understanding of who they are to be as well. We all benefit when women honor God by standing upright in dignity and confidence.

The Miracle of Unity and Mutual Respect

Your husband may catch the vision. Setting a personal etiquette as a couple absolutely complements your joint mission in life. Defining your personal etiquette together as a team opens wonderful conversations about which tender habits matter to each of you. Imagine the fellowship proceeding out of those kinds of marriage conversations!

Cultivating tender kindnesses to cherish and honor each other frees us to serve others. Plus, more trust and less drama means the momentum keeps building. Believe me, just like my dad, husbands can learn to treasure the tender courtesies we decide to habitually extend.

Plus, defining personal etiquette takes the edge off any arguments. While some heated discussion seems unavoidable, personal etiquette provides accountability both ways. Anticipating good manners, even in heated moments, strengthens your foundation of tenderness in marriage overall.

Because the standard is clear, you both learn to say, "I know that's not who you are, but your momentary lapse was hurtful." Eventually, positive thoughts replace negative assuming, stereotyping, and condemning.

What Will They Say at My Funeral?

Here's another tip for defining a personal etiquette: What do you want folks to say at your funeral? Of course, we can all be selfish sometimes. But since God designed you, you have hints in your heart's most joyful inclinations.

Perhaps you are the type of person who always has a kind word for everyone. You may stick up for the underdog. You may be a woman of conviction. Maybe you never miss a chance to create a blessing for others. Perhaps being outdoors or around animals is your greatest joy. You might be that woman who is gentle as a lamb with your children and grandchildren, but don't get between you and your cubs.

Are you the vulnerable, tender friend who openly shares the truth about what hurts or challenges you? Do you laugh at your own quirkiness? Perhaps, you always speak up in crucial moments when everyone else feels self-conscience. Whatever your personality, boundaries provided by a personal etiquette allow you to use your giftedness with joy in the kindest, most effective way.

Strengthening Each Other

Most married women are called upon to strengthen their husbands. Under ideal circumstances, God enhances unity by allowing us to strengthen each other. For example, in 1 Corinthians, Paul explains how God's Spirit unites us, bringing our various strengths and gifts together for the benefit of all, "There are diversities of gifts, but the same Spirit" (1 Corinthians 12:4).

When marriages function well, our mutual reliance on each other and respect attracts more loving relationships our way. Like a wedding ring's setting shows off gem-like beauty, your marriage should enhance both husband and wife, all your best qualities.

Please remember, a man who mistreats you messes with God's own daughter. I am not a trained therapist, but I know one thing for sure. Showing a lack of respect for you picks a fight with your Father. You are doing your husband no favors by tolerating behavior that challenges God's authority and power. Please seek the council of a wise cleric or therapist and the support of trustworthy friends as you make necessary changes. Abuse or safety issues may require you to seek immediate shelter and professional help.

In the long run, our personal etiquette will ensure a true trajectory for our family and life. For instance, by taking the car keys each time my dad had a drink, Mom clarified Dad's responsibility without ever scolding. She simply found the boundary and stuck with it. She kept us all safe, while simultaneously respecting his free will and providing gentle accountability.

Years later, through AA, he acknowledged Jesus and began to set a profound example of true humility. My mother waited years to see the impact his life had on countless people! But she had no guarantees the story would end the way it did.

No Personality Transplants

We're not looking for a personality transplant. We simply want to be the best expression of the person God created for His glory and joy. We want that for our hubby, too.

As you embrace your own unique design and calling, you'll recognize your husband's as well. His prescribed design deserves respect, even when he falters in offering respect to you. A personal etiquette allows you to be yourself and respect him.

I truly hope these ideas help you formulate a personal etiquette today for the place you are in your life right now. Please, drill deep in your own heart. Respecting ourselves means learning to trust our instincts. Defining a personal etiquette frees us to be our best selves. Without a doubt, I'm convinced we all truly know in our guts why we were designed.

When we listen for the whispers of our own heart, we hear the deepest yearnings, our truest inclinations. When we serve others wholeheartedly, we empower ourselves to ignore the naysayers and the rejectors. Blessedly, we sing and dance to the music God put in our hearts to worship Him. We learn to trust Him in ways beyond our comprehension. Our lives and marriages take on momentum fueled by self-respect and a sense of the eternal.

In Case You Were Wondering...

I gave up my personal impact to join together with his, so shouldn't our impact together weigh in with more sum total benefits to God's kingdom? I've wondered the same thing at times! Take heart. Even if we look at marriage as a simple accounting formula, God doesn't. Instead, God uses our relationships to bring others to Himself.

We can adopt the long view, trusting the power of the cross. There's a lot of confusion about God's will, but it boils down to this—He wants us to look as much like His Son as humanly possible. His will for us means rejoicing in Him, even while gently enforcing boundaries in our marriage via our own personal etiquettes.

Making an impact in the lives around us reminds me of climbing Mt. Kilimanjaro. How do people climb Mt. Kilimanjaro? With perseverance, with other people, and with humility, setting aside pride, and roughing it out in excruciatingly intimate circumstances. Did you know they only climb a few feet off the path to relieve their bowels when they trek up Mt. Kilimanjaro? Ugh! It's not pretty, and it's not easy.

You may never climb Kilimanjaro. Personally, I prefer vacations with restrooms. But, like climbing a mountain, authenticity is the key. *Do I know myself? Do I love myself? Am I willing to believe God loves me for who I am?* Just like climbing a mountain gets you the best view, hard work, good manners, vulnerability, and self-respect secure the privilege of being loved for who we are.

My prayer for us all is we hang tough with eternity in mind, knowing the unfailing love of our Father. In such courage, our lives will influence others in unexpected, eternal ways presently unforeseen by humans. Defining a personal etiquette will help.

Pause, Ponder, Pray, and then Proceed

Our truest inclination is enhanced by a personal etiquette. Even in the most trying moments in marriage, we can choose to respect ourselves. We can be upright. Ironically, knowing my best self sets my husband free to be his best self. Yep, weird how that works.

1. Understanding your needs: What good manners can you adopt to ensure you and your husband both feel safe in your relationship? List any new ideas about the benefits of etiquette. For example, if you need to ask your husband to forgive you for a bad habit—even a small one—please ask him. It's crazy, but apologies hold both people accountable.

2. Identifying your worth: When you fell in love with your husband, what was the etiquette like between you? In your own deepest heart, what are some bad habits and attitudes you need to improve? Choose a positive habit to reclaim from your early marriage and try it out again today.

3. Envisioning your future: Since God wants to personally equip you for success, in which relationship do you want a victory first? When you think of being kind in your home, what three habits come to mind? Write your three favorite family habits in a prominent place. Remember to thank your husband if any of those habits are his. I'll thank my hubby for the coffee he brought me this morning. If not, thank a close friend who encourages you with a habitual kindness. You could even write a note, a very cool thing to do for a friend!

My prayer for you, with my love

Dear God, we praise You, the One who delights in Your creation. You declare us Your crowning creation! We easily forget we are Your beloved daughters. It's easy to feel overwhelmed and competitive with our husbands. Please bless this beloved sister so she knows she can rest in the design You gave her. Give her words to express her commitment to a personal etiquette, reflecting who You are. Let her thank You for her husband's design with a tender and joyful heart. Help her hear the whispering of Your voice in her deepest heart.

Our hearts join together in this praise from Psalm 16:11: "You will show me the path of life; In Your presence *is* fullness of joy; At Your right hand *are* pleasures forever more."

To pray for yourself

Good Father, I seek You now in the quiet place. Please show me how You delight in me. Give me confidence that comes from knowing the truth (that I am precious in Your sight) and from doing what is hard (staying true to who I am in the midst of life's challenges).

When I am tempted to please my husband, rather than You, give me strength. Help me stay on course in my truest inclination. Give me a straight trajectory pointing to You. Allow me to drill deeply into my heart, drawing forth the best I have to offer. Energize me to express patience with myself and others. In all this, help me to generously love others from a strong place of confidence and grace. Bless me now because that's Your heart's desire. In Jesus' name I pray. Amen.

"Nothing is less important than which fork you use. Etiquette is the science of living. It embraces everything. It is ethics. It is honor." —**Emily Post**

CHAPTER ELEVEN

A Safe Place

How does creating a family purpose statement produce harmony?
By unifying us and equipping us to say no to distractions.

"This is a safe place," said our dear friend as he hugged David and me goodbye after a recent visit. I married into this friendship almost forty years ago. His casual comment landed in a soft spot in our hearts.

One of our goals in life was for our home to become a safe spot where others felt welcome and truly loved. When Dave and I married, we wanted to create a place where our family and friends could share their greatest frustrations and most personal fears and still feel loved.

Our friend's visits are always characterized by lots of joy, shared sorrows over the years, and the ebb and flow of many hours of honest conversation. As if that's not enough, sometimes he even brings bonus blessings, his beloved wife and son.

David and I struggled to communicate with each other, so we never thought of ourselves as masters of authentic conversation. How did we build a home life that allows folks to relax and be real? Accidentally, I guess.

Years ago, sometime in the early '90s, David decided our family needed a purpose statement, so he wrote one for us. I was not involved. Vision, purpose, and mission statements were rare for businesses back then. Who ever heard of writing one for a family? Honestly, the idea seemed crazy at the time, extreme to my way of thinking. Still, I went along with it because, well, what if it worked?

I pinned it to my bulletin board with a sigh and thought, if only. I added it to my prayer list of things I wished would be true for us someday. Somewhere along the way, probably in one of our many moves, I lost the scrap of paper.

Today, if you take any communications class in college, you may get these basic definitions of vision, purpose, and mission statements in your first lecture. I came to these late in life and had to figure them out for myself. That turned out to be a good thing, since there are various—often confusing—definitions floating around out there. Here are mine.

Vision: Why Make a Contribution?

First, a vision statement proclaims the big thing you and your team hope to contribute to the world. Vision answers the big why questions.[30] Why do you exist as an individual? Why will your marriage matter to anyone else? Why does your family exist?

Whatever your vision or dream, if it's so big it seems impossible, you are on the right track. Dream big. In fact, if you whisper your vision to a friend, you'll do it with a red face because it sounds crazy. At Camp Krafve, we exist to change the culture for pure good. Fortunately for us, we see God raising up lots of folks with the same dream, so our little part of the vision doesn't have to be daunting.

One clear vision statement belongs to Pine Cove Christian Camps, a camp well-known beyond East Texas where they are headquartered: "Pine Cove exists to be used by God to transform the lives of people for His purposes and His glory." If you saw their counselors in action each summer, you would know their vision transcends confusion. Young people arrive each summer enthusiastically united in their commitment to live transformative truth to God's glory. Unity

---

30 Brian Sooy, "The Difference Between Purpose, Mission, and Vision," https://www.aespire.com/blog/communications/the-difference-between-your-purpose-and-mission, accessed 02-10-20

around a shared vision reigns at Pine Cove.

The Bible offers a wonderful observation about the power of a vision, "Where there is no vision, the people perish" (Proverbs 29:18 KJV). The same verse is sometimes translated, "Where *there* is no revelation the people cast off restraint" (Proverbs 29:18). Personally, a little revelation and restraint in marriage seems like a blessing! Clarifying a vision for your family can be a powerful tool for unity. Sometimes vision and purpose statements blend together and that's okay. Basically, though, a purpose statement is an even more practical synopsis of your vision.

Purpose: What Hope Do You Offer Others?

Second, a purpose statement expresses the hope your family or business offers others. Purpose statements are even more functional than vision statements for unifying couples and families. Your purpose statement is how you intend to serve others; what you have to offer. Best of all, having a purpose gives positive focus to your life.

"For I know the thoughts that I think toward you, says the LORD, thoughts of peace and not of evil, to give you a future and a hope" (Jeremiah 29:11).

Believing God's thoughts toward us are positive gives direction and purpose to our lives. David's purpose statement went something like this, "The purpose of our family is to create a safe place, a home where people feel free and safe to be real and to know God the way He truly is."

Mission: How Do Your Practical Plans Look Today?

Third, a mission statement expresses the practical nuts and bolts of how you'll fulfill your vision and achieve your purpose in baby steps. Our mission at Camp Krafve is to produce as many positive messages as we can each week. The ways we do so may change over time. Presently, through Fireside Talk Radio, we catapult other peoples' messages out into the internet. With our books, we've added another layer of practical messages designed to help people enjoy healthy authentic communication.

When we adopt a mission for our family, it might feel overwhelming. But we're not doing anything alone. Plus, we take small steps daily. There are countless verses in the Bible about God's role of offering direction to our daily lives, but check out how He does it, from Proverbs 3:5–6.

"Trust in the LORD with all your heart, And lean not on your own understanding; In all your ways acknowledge Him, And He shall direct your paths."

We may choose a huge vision statement, then follow it with a giant purpose statement. It's a relief to know we can trust God with the path as we figure out what our mission is for today. One small conversation may be enough for one day, especially if our current mission is to foster a mutually rewarding marriage!

The Steady Power of Purpose

To say we wanted to create a safe family is pretty straightforward. But how would we convey our acceptance and love to people who disagreed with our values? What if our own kids rejected our ideas? Or an aging parent challenged our patience? David and I faced a myriad of challenges along the way trying to stay true to our mission each day.

Later, we added the vision statement. Anybody can say they want to influence a culture for pure good. The actual task seems overwhelming. Fortunately, influencing the culture for good is a vision we share with many others. Our big vision statement reminds us to work well with those who share our grand dream. Remembering our vision, purpose, and mission always helps us stay steady.

Here's another example of how the three statements relate to each other. My toddling granddaughter may dream of eating. She may open the pantry door and think of how great it would be to eat. That's her vision. She may make suggestions to me about food. Her designated purpose is to get me to help her eat. But the fact is, she'll be hungry until we slather peanut butter on the bread. She must then put it in her mouth, chew it up, and swallow it. Her mission statement revolves around the peanut butter on the bread in her hand and mouth.

How will we accomplish our vision and purpose? With a mission statement, we can spotlight the immediate path along the way.

Businesses, churches, nonprofits, and families often change their purpose and mission statements as needs change. For instance, a young couple may agree their vision or dream is to create fellowship in as many ways as possible for a lifetime. They may decide their purpose is to create a home for their children. For now, though, their mission may be as simple as keeping their toddlers in clean diapers, while finding time to grab a bite with another young family each month.

David gets kudos here for imagining a big purpose for our family when no one else got it. By no one, I mean, ahem, me. To create a place where we could be real meant being vulnerable about what did not work well. Most of the time, for me at least, the process of being vulnerable, does not feel safe at all. Actually, vulnerability—getting real—sounds downright scary.

Even though I thought he was crazy, my husband was right. We all need a place to retreat where we feel safe to be real. Creating a family purpose statement set a course for our family that unifies us still. In spite of our ongoing communication mess-ups, David and I shared a sense of purpose.

Nonprofits and businesses use purpose and mission statements constantly to keep their teams true to the long-term vision, so why not couples? Our youngest daughter was so taken with the idea she created her own vision statement while she was still a single gal working on her MBA: "To have as big of a positive impact on as many people as I possibly can." I am including hers so you can see how varied purpose statements pop up even in the same family.

When I asked her if I could quote her in this book, she sent me back this reply, "Yes, but now I joke about just wanting to have a positive impact on five people (being my children)." Purpose statements definitely change, especially when the reality of life forces us to stay practical.

Personally, I like the idea of creating a vision statement for a family right away. Vision statements can unify a couple and their family around the long-term dream. When we think about our vision statement and what we want to contribute to the world we live in, we should dream big.

Then, creating a purpose statement can shed light on short-term goals. For instance, knowing our family wants to affect the culture for good inspires our purpose statement to create a safe place to honor God's true nature. When our kids were small, our purpose of honoring God in a safe home inspired us to complete the tasks (our day's mission) required to meet the physical, emotional, and spiritual needs of our kids.

For David and me now, this week's mission might include bill paying, creating new blogs, interviewing a guest for a podcast, and spending time with the grandchildren. Today, I'm working on my next book. Later, I'll reward myself by reading my friend's new book. Every activity relates back to providing a safe place for people to know God as He truly is and reaching a culture desperately in need of hope.

You can see how a mission statement puts the daily fine print on how to fulfill your big vision and accomplish your purpose. Back then, we accomplished our day's mission in a thousand ways each day, starting with tying our kids' shoes and brushing their hair. Now, with grown children, our daily mission has shifted to new ways of creating and promoting positive, life-affirming messages.

Vision? Purpose? Mission? Give Me a Break!

Does all this seem a little over the top for non-communication majors? You may decide you don't need all three statements. It's okay to give yourself a break. You may skip all three forever. Or focus on only one for now. We didn't know the difference back when David started by creating our purpose statement.

May I recommend focusing on the purpose statement if you decide to try only one? A purpose statement will immediately make deciding your priorities for your day easier. Whatever you do, don't miss the chance to talk over vision, purpose, and mission with your spouse. Just talking about these kinds of statements will galvanize the foundational unity you share.

Nailing down a clear, one-sentence statement by which to measure every decision frees and empowers couples. If you approach the process gently, it's a safe, nonthreatening way to practice good communication as a couple. It doesn't have to be difficult. Both purpose and mission can be condensed into one sentence. Simple is better. Your mission statement can be a family motto you never have to share with anyone else unless you want to.

In fact, devising your own purpose statement will set a good trajectory for your life as a couple. A purpose statement can evolve into a lifelong vision, as David's original purpose statement has for our family.

Additionally, you can use your family purpose statement as a benchmark to validate your personal etiquette. Purpose statements may evolve over time; you can always change it later as your family's needs change. Businesses frequently change theirs as they reassess their purpose. Personally, I'm enjoying how our youngest daughter's daily mission evolves now that she has a family, given her vision statement.

Skydiving, Bungee Jumping, Risk Taking

To a large extent, creating your own personal purpose statement as a couple cuts through the clutter. With such clarity, you feel free to say no to stuff that isn't going to get you down the road toward your life's purpose. For instance, here's an example of how a simple statement can clarify your decisions. Somewhere along the way, Dave and I realized as entrepreneurs we took enough risk, we sure don't need anymore. So, we often remind each other, "We don't do danger for entertainment."

Skydiving and bungee jumping were never big temptations for us because we both agreed those activities have nothing to do with creating a safe place for folks to know God in a real and vulnerable way. It's only fair to confess, I was a little tempted when President Bush parachuted out of a plane for his birthday.

Some of the best decisions Dave and I made along the way started with the word no. People around us thought we were crazy sometimes, but our culture spins out of control with distractions and activities. Sometimes our imaginations need to rest and re-spark. Like the pilot light on a furnace, imagination burns out if we neglect it.

Plus, your marriage needs quiet moments. We all need unplugged down time. No screens allowed. By pushing pause, we give ourselves the best gift of all, a quiet moment to relish together. Great marriage conversations are much more likely in quiet, relaxed moments.

For that reason alone, discussing a family purpose statement is a risk worth taking. We want to take risks when it comes to trying new communication strategies in our marriage. But it's okay to measure the risk and scale it back when necessary, especially to create down time. Having a purpose statement helps us decide when the time is right for a little managed risk taking. Maybe someday I will jump out of an airplane. Thankfully, today is not the day.

By taking a moment to clarify life's big purpose for you as a couple, you set yourselves up to arrive at your long-term destination together. Jointly, you clarify and negotiate the path you choose to follow. Your purpose statement may begin to crystalize into a bigger vision for your future together. If you choose to create a mission statement, it can provide daily recurring checkpoints. I hope your hubby joins you in the process. But even if, like my husband, you have to do it alone, you'll be glad you focused your attention on a purpose for your family.

In Case You Were Wondering…

What if I want to have a big family purpose, but my husband doesn't get it? I hope you do what David did and write it down anyway. By writing it down, David allowed me time to process what I didn't understand. Without ever saying a word, his actions invited me to pray through it. Plus, writing things down lets us see when our prayers are answered. By the way, God does things all the time that our husbands (or we) don't get.

A purpose statement creates unity around a big idea. David and I both think safety is a big deal, so safety showed up in our purpose statement. Safety is often a deal breaker when a woman doesn't feel safe in a relationship. Men need safety, too, as the Scripture points out: "The heart of her husband safely trusts her" (Proverbs 31:11). Feeling safe allowed David and me to finally relax and share our real inner self.

In creating family purpose statements, start by focusing on the things you agree on. Please go ahead and start a conversation, even if you come to no conclusion right away. Your process will itself be informative. Then accommodate anything else, even if it's a point of disagreement. You can return to any uncomfortable points later.

Be prepared to flex when your statement needs to evolve. If you find only one big point of agreement, praise God! You just stumbled onto the big idea to unite and inspire you both.

Pause, Ponder, Pray, and then Proceed

God has a plan for you and, if you are married, it includes honoring and serving His kingdom in your marriage. Does honoring Him as the purpose for your marriage seem like an impossible miracle? Remember, miracles are God's specialty!

1. Understanding your needs: To formulate your own purpose statement, answer this question: Why did you get married in the first place? Are you a person who loves a direct path or can you appreciate a meandering scenic route? What kind of person is your hubby? Take a minute to write down some of the things you loved about being a couple when you first married.

2. Identifying your worth: In what ways can you support your husband like no one else? As a special research project, email ten people you respect, tell them what you admire about their marriages. Then ask what they see as beneficial about your marriage. Capture their responses. Perhaps, you just created your next anniversary gift without spending a penny!

3. Envisioning your future: What do you enjoy together that could become your best and brightest joint contribution to your world? What was the last thing you did together that blessed you both and someone else? Write down the date and the blessings that came from that encounter. Now, think of a few ways to expand the joy of contributing good things to our world.

My prayer for you, with my love

Dear God, please bless my sister with a sense of Your purpose in her marriage. We all feel distracted and divided in our own homes sometimes, Lord. We praise You together because throughout history we see Your providential hand guiding Your people. We are not helpless. You set us on a sure path. When we arrive at our destination, we will find ourselves in Your glorious presence. Give this dear sister patience and steadfastness as she travels. May she abide in Your presence in complete peace and joy, as she fulfills Your purpose for her today.

Let Psalm 17 be ever on our lips, "I have called upon You, for You will hear me, O God; Incline Your ear to me, *and* hear my speech. Show Your marvelous lovingkindness by Your right hand, O You who save those who trust *in You* from those who rise up *against them*" (verses 6–7).

To pray for yourself

Good Father, You are the One who called me for Your purpose. I desire to be undistracted and farsighted. Therefore, I turn to You. Teach me Your ways that I may walk in them, O Lord. Give my husband's heart what he needs for today. Rather than feeling outnumbered or divided in my home, help me ask for the support I need from my husband, family, and friends. As a couple, give us words to express Your purpose for our marriage. O Lord, teach me to speak with clarity about our future together. I want to be a wife who finds unity with my husband in Your purpose. Bless me now because that's Your heart's desire. In Jesus' name I pray. Amen.

"A small body of determined spirits fired by an unquenchable faith in their mission can alter the course of history." — **Mahatma Gandhi**

CHAPTER TWELVE

Keeping What We Give Away

How does welcoming others
instruct our own hearts?
By teaching us that we, too, are worthy of welcome.

All my files lost! The computer glitch of a writer's worst nightmares! Frantically searching my emails for attachments, I soon discovered—since I freely share everything I write—my account contained copies of anything important. I easily downloaded all my favorite articles via attachments. My giant computer fail highlighted the direct correlation between giving and keeping.

In another striking example, when our son was born, my friend Joan showed up one day with a one-of-a-kind baby gift. Imagine my delight when I opened the package and discovered two tiny treasures from among keepsakes she saved from her sons' nursery.

Her gift remains one of my all-time favorites. She gave me a gift of herself. I cherished the bib and her antique plaque. But only for a short time. Within months, I received a startling phone call one morning.

"Cathy, there was a fire at Joan's house last night. Everyone is safe."

The scene was surreal. Only a charred, blackened slab remained of her once beautiful two-story home overlooking the lake, a masterpiece of contemporary architecture, designed by a colleague of Frank Lloyd Wright. The insurance company made an initial payment immediately. Within days, Joan's family settled into a rental house with a convenient barn out back for storing the sooty remains of her life.

I showed up a few days later with a casserole and the bib and the plaque. She welcomed me in a tender embrace. Then she toured me through her rental house like it was an estate. Once family heirlooms graced the rooms, replaced now by practical pieces, like desks from Walmart for her sons.

"Can you believe God found us a rental house with a barn in back to put everything!" Against all odds, with her beautiful home a smoking mess, she proclaimed God as the One who took care of her family. When she opened the big doors to the barn, the pungent smell of charcoal slammed us. Gratefully, she pointed out she did not have to store the rubber tubs containing the smelly remains of her life inside her rental house. As we applied cleansers to her elegant china to salvage what little remained, she rejoiced, discovering freedom in letting go of material things.

Joyfully, she shared how God preserved what was important, burning away all else. She was grateful for her family's safety, but God's provision showed up in the small stuff. For instance, the loss of her sons' baby pictures grieved her most. Fortunately, Joan extravagantly shared pictures of her children with extended family over the years. Literally, the same pictures she gave away came back to her after the fire. Her emotional well-being and joy in that trying moment affected me forever. I learned from Joan we only keep what we give away. I like the way Luke describes the blessing of giving.

"Give, and it will be given to you: good measure, pressed down, shaken together, and running over will be put into your bosom. For with the same measure that you use, it will be measured back to you" (Luke 6:38). The Scriptures remind us again and again our hearts only keep what we give away. Welcoming others with a hospitable heart is the best kind of gift. God Himself does the same for each of us.

Hospitable Hearts

The principle of giving and keeping applied to Joan's pictures, but it especially applies to relationships. When we share joy and generosity in life, we quickly learn the correlation of giving and keeping. Certainly, we've all seen memes announcing the best way to have a friend is to be one. In marriage, the principle of giving and keeping manifests itself again in hospitality. Hospitality is the art of welcoming others into your heart, as well as your home.

The hospitable host embraces guests with joy. He graciously offers them refreshment, something prepared with loving attention, putting everyone at ease. Inviting them to relax, he offers momentary respite from the day's ordinary struggles. With a smile and gracious laughter, he sets the tone for an evening of intimate friendship and togetherness. Often, hospitality includes a chance to celebrate, perhaps a graduation, a baby's birth, or an engagement announcement.

Hospitality stretches to include more than simply hosting parties. True hospitality of the heart isn't bound to a location or an event. Instead, true hospitality welcomes strangers into our lives with tender openness and understanding. No one should lack companionship; our hearts instinctively tell us so. Therefore, by welcoming others into our lives, we affirm their value to God. By welcoming others enthusiastically, we demonstrate how God rejoices over each one us with delight.

Enthusiastic Love

Even a chance encounter can be an opportunity to display God's enthusiastic love. I intentionally model my greetings after a blessed friend who consistently greets me with extravagant joy. Sometimes people are put off by my extravagant way of greeting them, so I take a step back to give them room. I try to stick with it in general, though. My friend's constant delight in our friendship inspires me. Bewildering people with extravagant joy about their presence is not necessarily a bad thing.

The principle of giving and keeping applies to all relationships, not only guests, close friends, or chance encounters. Sometimes at home we forget to treat family members with the same deference we give strangers. Especially in our homes, welcoming our most beloved family members reflects God's joy in their presence.

In marriage, by consistently making a husband feel welcome with an open heart, we express the giving and keeping principle perfectly, even when it costs us. We've all experienced moments in our marriage when it felt costly to be kind.

Let's face it, in marriage, we can get worn down and discouraged trying to keep our hearts open. Our closest relationships can hurt momentarily when they hit a snag. Or certain areas may be sticking points for years due to unexamined wounds or baggage. A husband's wounded heart may create unavoidable difficulties in a marriage and family.

Fortunately, the giving and keeping principle unfolds in a beautiful blessing, especially in those most difficult circumstances. Let me explain what I mean.

Deep unity is based on the principle that we only keep what we give away. Everyone wants to be welcomed into a safe, happy relationship. But sometimes, the most difficult person to welcome is the person we love the most. Why? Because hurt, resentments, and unforgiveness can stack up until we can scarcely cherish one another.

Miraculously, the person who chooses to offer a welcoming heart to a spouse, in spite of circumstances, affirms God's welcoming love for both people. Fascinating. As is so often the case, when we give God His due, He returns it to us. In other words, we get to experience the love we gave away to someone else! Cathy, you ask, how can that possibly be true? It sounds too far-fetched!

Here's how. Welcoming others into a safe and affirming environment frees us to realize we deserve the same kind of love. When we express God's love for another person by welcoming them enthusiastically into our lives, we simultaneously teach our own hearts to trust in His exuberant love for us. What a fabulous little mini-miracle created by the giving and keeping principle!

Different Styles of Welcome

God demonstrates His grand plan for us daily, if we but pay attention. As we marvel at His design of others, we get a peek at His satisfaction with our own design. If your husband lacks understanding about welcoming folks, so be it. You owe it to yourself to affirm God's love for you by treating him with enthusiastic kindness.

Your husband's way of welcome may be a mystery to you simply because it's different from yours. Understanding his expression of kindness may be a matter of asking a few thoughtful questions to communicate clearly. We all have different ways of welcoming others into our lives.

I am a natural extrovert, so my daily adventures involve friends I just met. Since David is more of an introvert, his favorite way to welcome people is in small numbers to our home where he can focus his attention and connect. Does it matter if the style best suited to you is different still? No.

Fortunately for me, almost from the moment I became a Christian, I heard Bill Bright mention God's divine appointments. From then on, I quit believing in accidental encounters. Instead, I began welcoming others in joyful anticipation of what God might do as a blessing for both of us.

God is not looking for those who will patronize others with false affection. We are not offering a welcome to get something out of it. Instead, when God is in the process, everyone gets a blessing. Our decision to practice generous hospitality of the heart is rewarded by a God who loves us. We do it to honor Him because we want to reflect His character. What a wonderful bonus when He blesses us as a result of our tribute to Him!

Rejection: Powerful Force for Destruction

Welcoming hospitality of the heart is a powerful force for togetherness. Rejection, on the other hand, is one of the most powerful forces for evil on the planet. (Imagine that in Darth Vader's voice). We all want to practice welcoming people with joy as opposed to rejecting them.

I realize as I write many women are in seemingly impossible situations in their marriages. Please let me welcome you into the secret society of women who hang in there, making small changes in the hope of better days ahead. While you pray and ponder, may I offer you one more thought? Please keep yourself safe. God has prequalified you to be a woman of influence. It is His intention to use you in many lives. But He can only use you on this earth if you protect yourself from danger, especially in your home.

Our pastor likes to remind us, "People are messy." It's especially tempting to subtly reject messy people, even shunning them. In our marriages, we toss out subtle rejection, like beauty queens toss candy from parade floats. We may even accept subtle rejections and shunning as a natural part of normal marriage until one day our emotional reservoir dries up. Suddenly, we encounter a big marital mess because we forgot the habit of cherishing each other.

One example of a habitual form of rejection includes subtle bullying. Bullying gets a lot of attention now among students. But we want to be alert for it in our adult relationships, too.

In spite of all the education done on the topic, I still hear parents say a youngster "brought it on himself." Without knowing it, they are saying that the social ineptitude of the student being bullied justifies rejection.

Bullying is a serious topic. I like the definition that Tina Meier shared when I interviewed her for Fireside Talk Radio: "The definition of bullying includes three essential components. 1) Bullying is an aggressive behavior involving unwanted, negative actions. 2) Bullying involves a pattern of repeated behaviors over time. 3) Bullying involves an imbalance of power or strength."[31]

Because bullying can be so subtle, we women may not recognize when bullying creeps into our marriages or other relationships. We may even feel we brought it on ourselves. If other people cut us off without listening to our opinions, that may be a form of bullying. If we are subtly demeaned with humor or our feelings are minimized, that may be bullying. Any threat, like "you won't like it when," is bullying. Sometimes, bullying figuratively smacks us in the face, like when someone says, "That's not a threat; it's a promise."

The wife who receives more rejection than welcome can begin to question the authenticity of anyone's welcome, no matter how warm.

---

31 Tina Meier, Fireside Talk Radio, "Bullying in School, Her Wisdom with Tina Meier, How to Help Our Kids," 02-04-19.

What a serious and painful problem to experience! Mood swings and inconsistency can be another form of bullying.

We don't want to be hypersensitive or check our sense of humor at the door, but please be aware of intense, but subtle rejection. Seek out friends who offer you sincere, consistent welcome because God wants to use them in your life to confirm your worth. What a contrast a warm welcome is to those suffering from rejection!

The Sorrow and Suffering of Rejection

A familiar Bible verse reminds us of what powerful force rejection wields. When dear friends experienced a death in their family, I Googled "a Man of sorrows and acquainted with grief" so I could write it on a sympathy card. Taking a closer look at this prophetic verse, its context surprised me. Rejection defined Jesus' suffering.

"He is despised and rejected by men, A Man of sorrows and acquainted with grief. And we hid, as it were, *our* faces from Him; He was despised, and we did not esteem Him" (Isaiah 53:3).

Rejection is a form of suffering deeply associated with Jesus' cross. When we think of all the ways Jesus suffered leading up to His death on the cross, we usually think of the whipping, the crown of thorns, the nails in His hands and feet, etc. If we're spiritual, we may perceive the suffering invoked by our sin. Clearly, though, this verse states that Jesus suffered intensely because of rejection.

Bullying is just one form of rejection. In another example, giving our husbands the cold shoulder represents the opposite of a warm welcome. To hide our faces, like mentioned in the above verse, is to shun. Shunning cuts off the other person from our relationship. Control issues, coercion, self-rejection, and victimhood are closely attached to shunning. We can exercise compassion for those who shun us because they truly suffer themselves.

Other subtle but excruciating forms of rejection may include talking negatively about each other to your children or parents, criticizing each other in public, or challenging parental authority in front of others. Failing to esteem each other constitutes rejection.

Because rejection qualifies as suffering, it's the first thing we need to eliminate from our marriages. We want to develop an attitude of welcome for each other. How does it look when we esteem each other? Ah, now we've circled back to that wonderful little word *cherished!*

Ice Cream Bars and a Hearty Welcome

My son begged to visit one couple in our neighborhood who kept ice cream bars in the freezer for him. Grinning with happiness, they never failed to greet us with hearty handshakes, welcoming us into their cozy kitchen. Their neighborly welcome set the tone for warm friendship and fond memories still cherished today. We have all stood on a favorite neighbor's front porch, waiting for that moment when the door swings open.

Being safe in marriage begins with welcoming each other into our private domain where we choose vulnerability. Warmly we receive each other, safe from rejection. Ignore me if this doesn't apply, but I think the occasional ice cream bar is genius!

In order to welcome each other in marriage, we need time together. Careless use of our time threatens marriages. You already know I'm a failure at date nights, but intimacy requires we carve out special time for each other. Freely defining your quiet time together still requires you to set aside distractions. Fortunately, having a purpose statement and a personal etiquette helps us safeguard our priorities, especially time with a spouse. Purposefully choosing to spend our time relevantly makes sense for today's modern woman, especially when we consider how important it is to have a hospitable heart toward our hubby.

When we say no to low priorities, we free ourselves to say yes to our most important commitments and most beloved people. With our priorities and purpose spelled out, we can welcome others into our lives based on God's example of unfailing love for us. Freely, we can generously and compassionately spend time based on our priorities. All the while we give ourselves complete freedom to say no when we need to reserve private time for ourselves. In fact, we freely forego some relationships altogether because the amount of care involved distracts us from God's purpose for our lives. What freedom!

When welcoming others, even in their messiest moments, we look past their pain and see worthiness. Soon we look forward to unique people with the fresh perspectives they offer. We may find ourselves laughing hilariously due to the unexpected people and surprising viewpoints populating our lives. Sooner or later, we learn to treasure tender moments with people who trust us with their most vulnerable spots.

This blessing ricochets back to our own hearts, deepening our fellowship with everyone we know. Why? Because we soon root ourselves in the knowledge that we deserve welcome, too. We see our own perspectives as valuable, especially when they're unique. We come to view our own uniqueness as a surprising gift. Instead of seeing ourselves as weird or out of step with others, we view ourselves as interesting and exceptional.

Then, in growing confidence, we start to see our own vulnerabilities as blessings to be shared authentically. Soon, we gain even more energy for welcoming others. We let go of distractions and insecurities. Why? Because we believe God cherishes each one of us. Consequently, it's easier to remember a husband needs welcome, especially from his wife.

Giving and Keeping Joy

My friend Paula told me another story that illustrates the truth about how we only keep what we give away. When her family made their first trip to Ethiopia, they felt overwhelmed by all the physical needs going unmet daily. Their hearts began to imagine how they could joyfully welcome new Ethiopian friends into their lives over the coming years. As they were packing to return home, her husband suddenly flipped over his suitcase and dumped all the contents on the bed.

"We are giving this all away," he announced with excitement. Knowing how Americans travel, I easily imagine a suitcase stuffed with blue jeans, T-shirts, a few dress shirts, slacks, and several pairs of shoes, all things of extreme value in a neighborhood where people often go hungry and barefoot. Greater still was the joyous love he expressed.

Imagine the hilarious excitement later as they tossed items across a big room crowded with new friends who gathered to see them off to the airport. "Who wants this shirt? Who needs flip flops?" Because of her husband's spontaneous generosity, Paula and her family left with empty suitcases but full hearts. They gave away the peripherals and kept joy instead.

Her husband's example reminds us of how hilariously fun it can be to give of ourselves. Fellowship flourishes all around in the sunshine of such generosity of spirit. I love Paula's story about her husband's initiating leadership! We, too, can empty our bags of peripherals and fill our hearts with hilarious joy.

How wonderful to free ourselves of baggage by living open, generous, and vulnerable lives! We can have a heart that welcomes others. As we joyfully welcome others, we affirm our own worthiness, even in our messiest moments. Consequently, we practice welcoming all those we love into a rich circle of fellowship, beginning in our own hearts.

In Case You Were Wondering...

We are so busy; what happens if we don't welcome others? Some women appear to keep an open, hospitable heart naturally. Some don't. I'll let you in on a secret, though. Welcoming is a learned skill, resulting in tremendous reward. As we learn to welcome others, we claim it for our own hearts.

No matter our personality, welcoming others helps us understand how much we yearn for welcome, too. For instance, if we don't carve out some time for others, an introvert spouse will wither. An extrovert spouse will resent the lack of a social life. However, as we welcome others, we learn to trust our good Father to receive us as well.

Not everybody gets great parents. Remember we are all messy sometimes. We honor God when we exercise compassion for adults who seem messy. In doing so, we coach our own kids to maintain compassion and healthy boundaries.

At one point, David and I finally labeled Sunday afternoon as sacred. We were worn out and needed time marked off exclusively for our family. Maybe you feel too busy because you are too busy. It's fine to get off the fast track and pace ourselves.

By the way, being busy is substantially different than living a full-throttle life devoted to God's priorities. He always prioritizes time for rest. Now that's good time management, allowing us to welcome all people with energy, joy, and appropriate boundaries.

Pause, Ponder, Pray, and then Proceed

Don't you love to see toddlers run to their daddies, laughing with joy? I thought my favorite memory was when our kids would jump up and throw themselves into Dave's arms. But now our grandchildren run to their dads, laughing with joy. I'm collecting favorite memories by the bucket loads! Together, let's welcome our good Father with unrestrained, childlike joy now.

1. Understanding your needs: Take a minute to define on paper what rejection looks like to you. Most couples notice right away where they differ. How do your opposite perspectives bring a balance to your life?

What are your five favorite attributes of your husband? In Texas we use the word *simpatico* to describe natural like-mindedness. In what ways are you simpatico with your hubby?

2. Identifying your worth: What seems to be the way your friends count on you? Make a list to remind yourself of your impact. Start a collection of thank-you notes saved from friends over the years to review when you need a pick-me-up. When I need a boost, the kind truthful words of friends help me.

3. Envisioning your future: If you could eliminate all rejection, what would your marriage look like? What miracle would you ask of a God who welcomes you into His presence? How could your welcome for your husband look this evening? Since no one seems to write real notes anymore, why not write a short note to your hubby naming one special reason you married him in the first place.

My prayer for you, with my love

Dear God, You receive my sister with joy. Strengthen her against those moments when we all feel disconnected. Bless her with friends and children who become skilled with her in this heart discipline of welcome. Surround her with bright energy for giving away hilarious welcome to any and all You send her way. Teach her to order her steps and manage her time. Surprise her with relationships You have picked out for her, like a lover picks out a bright diamond for his beloved. Let her glory in Your wholehearted welcome.

Together we rejoice with these words from Psalm 17, "Keep me as the apple of Your eye; Hide me under the shadow of Your wings, From the wicked who oppress me, *From* my deadly enemies who surround me. …As for me, I will see Your face in righteousness; I shall be satisfied when I awake in Your likeness" (verses 8–9, 15).

To pray for yourself

Lord Jesus, You are the One who walked this earth with crowds following You. They loved You one moment and rejected You the next. You are the One who keeps loving me no matter who rejects me. The Bible identifies rejection as Your suffering. Teach me to love as You love. Help me put aside rejection and welcome others, knowing I am worthy of Your delight. Rather than wallowing in isolation, help me look for ways to embrace a lifestyle of collaboration. As You and I go along together, allow me to patiently and tenderly pass along Your effervescent welcome to my husband with joy. Bless me now because that's Your heart's desire. In Your name I pray. Amen.

"The only things we can keep are the things we freely give to God. What we try to keep for ourselves is just what we are sure to lose."
—C.S. Lewis, *Mere Christianity*

Dad Makes Amends

How does forgiveness equip us to listen honestly?
*When we take responsibility for our own mistakes,
we find compassion to listen with integrity.*

When Dad had been in Alcoholics Anonymous for a while, I noticed he was beginning to make amends with the people in his life. Making amends is Step 8 of the Twelve Steps, a program of AA. Here it is from the Big Book, as we affectionately call it: "8.) Made a list of all persons we had harmed, and became willing to make amends to them all."[32]

Naturally, I wondered when he would get around to me. When he invited me to lunch so he could make amends with me, I was ready. In typical fashion for Dad, he took me to a nice steak place. We sat across from each other at a cozy, quiet table.

"What's on your mind?" he asked.

"I have abandonment and trust issues I think I inherited from you, and I am having a hard time shaking them," I answered, jumping right in.

By then, I knew some of Dad's story. His father was in Italy immediately behind the front lines, a physician patching up soldiers during WWII. Grandpa was awarded a Purple Heart for an injury sustained

---

32 Alcoholics Anonymous, *The Story of How Many Thousands of Men and Women Have Recovered from Alcoholism*. Third Edition (Alcoholics Anonymous World Services, Inc., New York, 1976) p.59

when shrapnel pierced his helmet, injuring him, but leaving his ability to think intact. Dad's older brother was in medical school in Galveston, rushed along at seventeen by a military in need of doctors.

My dad was at home in Austin with his mother and his grandmother as his dad served overseas and his older brother trained to join the fight. As a seven-year-old boy, my dad cared for his grandmother who was bedridden and probably in need of hospice care. I believe his love of medicine and desire to cure people began there. In the days before we used the term "mental health," his mother began to have hallucinations. Dad's own abandonment issues stemmed back to that time. Up and down his street folks were holding it together on the home front while the men fought in Europe and the Pacific. Stoicism reigned in neighborhoods all across America.

As we talked, Dad tenderly acknowledged my hurt and asked me to forgive him. Then he surprised me with a story I treasure to this day.

"You remember the cemetery where Granny is buried, don't you?" he asked. I sure did. We buried her on an overcast day when a light frosting of snow fell as if from heaven. Snow rarely happens in Austin, Texas.

He told me how he and my tenderhearted mom went to the cemetery together after he joined AA. There, he poured out his grief and hurt over his mother's gravestone, with my mother holding him as he cried. Dad asked his mother to forgive him for the bitterness and anger he carried from his childhood. He grieved because his mother died before he sobered up enough to face his hurt. At her graveside, Dad forgave his mother for the circumstances of his childhood she could not control. He let his hurt go.

Sometimes we simply offer mercy and grace and forgiveness because we can. We don't get to judge. Because forgiveness is essential to our own survival, we forgive. Dad was not finished surprising me, though.

"What's next?" he asked.

"That's it, Dad. I think that's enough, don't you?"

Slowly, he took a piece of paper out of his pocket and unfolded it. First, he looked quizzically at his paper. Then, he studied me. He looked down at his paper again.

"But I have a list, and there are seventy-nine more things on it," he said sheepishly.

Seventy-nine more things. You have got to be kidding.

"Well, we could go through it item by item, and I could forgive you for each one. Or we could just forget the rest of the list. Obviously, if it was ever important, I've already forgiven you, Dad."

Dad paused for minute. I could see he was thinking hard. Then he folded up his list, put it back in his pocket, and said something profoundly appropriate for our family. "Let's order dessert!" he announced, rubbing his hands together in anticipation.

Dad made amends to me any way he could, that day and in the days to come. In reality, though, amends began long before our meeting. From his fifties on, Dad worked at his own recovery. I began to see him as a marvelous example of what integrity and humility look like in the inner person.

When Others Sin

Sometimes, a husband may hurt us to the point we wonder if we can recover. *How do I forgive my husband?* In my experience, the pain inflicted by a husband's actions proportionately match the wife's response. If you are feeling extremely hurt, your gut is trying to tell you something.

There is one exception. In the case of repetitive hurts, our response may seem crazy. Repetitive hurts tend to grow in their pain quotient. Therefore, if the pain seems off the chart in comparison to the injury, repetition is probably the culprit. You may be experiencing extreme pain in response to a pattern of small but habitual slights.

For instance, I notice my anger is still occasionally disproportionate to some small slight. Such disproportionate anger means I've ignored small pain over a matter of time. When I overreact, I need to have a tender conversation with David before I blow my stack again. A quick review of boundaries may prevent future issues.

But perhaps you tolerated severe pain for a long time for the sake of your children. Especially with an ex-husband in the picture, forgiveness can be excruciating. In fact, much of the suffering in marriage—and divorce—comes out of a habit of slow rejection and hard-heartedness.

Some wounds are deep and complicated, perhaps dating back several generations in family backgrounds. Actively pursuing healing by seeking counseling with clergy or a professional will help.

God designed you to be a victor, not a victim (Romans 8:37). In fact, God designed you to wear many hats, but the victim hat is not one we want to adopt as a regular part of our wardrobe. Therefore, stay alert for the many ways God shows up in your pain to comfort you, particularly using wise women. Look for small changes you can make along the way to bring you out of the deep pain and grief you may feel.

Remember, Jesus' greatest suffering was rejection. Forgiveness in marriage is perhaps the most difficult challenge. Fortunately, three terrific incentives to forgive exist, 1) the freedom we desire for our own futures, 2) if we are parents, the example we set for our kids' futures, and 3) the example we set for those who do not know Jesus yet.

One wise friend asked me, "Isn't God commanding us to forgive a good incentive?" Okay, it probably should be, but in my ole hard-hearted, stubborn self, commands tend to bristle my spine. I find I have to remind myself how much He loves me and wants what is best for me. Then, my prideful heart softens and I remember whom I serve.

In the Lord's prayer, Jesus taught us to pray to God for forgiveness because He knows what is best for us and He loves us (Matthew 6:9–13). But that doesn't mean forgiveness is easy. Please know you are worthy of a life free from unforgiveness because of the value God places on your life. Jesus willingly paid the ultimate price for you, so you can live free of self-condemnation and denial, unshackled from self-righteousness.

Additionally, in the case of adultery for instance, you alone are in the position to prayerfully decide what will be best for your future. Many people around you may tell you what you should do. They may even put a false guilt trip on you. You alone, along with your good Father and your husband, know the details of what led to any crisis in your marriage. Well-meaning Christian friends may judge and condemn. You may be called on to forgive them for judging what they do not understand.

If your husband breaks your vows and initiates another relationship founded on sexual intercourse, your goal is to forgive your husband eventually. For your own sake, you will want to let go of any bitterness stemming from the injustice he inflicted on you. Forgiveness is essential for your own health. God commands us to forgive because He wants what is best for us.

If you make unwise decisions that threaten your marriage and family, you may need to ask forgiveness of God, your husband, and perhaps others. You may need to forgive yourself.

Whether or not you decide to try to rebuild the marriage you first formed is entirely up to you. No other human has the right to judge the decision you make. No one else has enough information to judge your situation wisely, no matter what they think they know. Feel free to disregard human condemnation and seek wisdom and healing from God and wise, trustworthy friends, even professionals.

Denial: Refusing to Admit a Mess

One of the biggest obstacles to forgiveness is denial. Denial is when a person refuses to admit he or she messed up. We've all experienced denial in some way or another.

I know sometimes in modern terms, denial means to keep our head in the sand about somebody else's sin. I especially like what Debra L. Butterfield writes in her book *Carried by Grace*, "I didn't want to believe my husband could do such a vile thing. Nonetheless, I did accept it. Refusal to believe a problem actually exists despite evidence to the contrary is denial, and carried to extremes can cause psychological issues. Denial doesn't make the situation go away. Once a traumatic situation is accepted, we can resolve to take appropriate action to make things better."

The Holy Spirit wants to whisper comfort in our hurting hearts when other people's sin impacts us and our families. I understand we experience a protective initial shock whenever crisis strikes. But if we stay in denial about our true circumstances, we imply God is unable to help us when we need Him most.

When we fail to truthfully acknowledge someone else's sin, we've done them no favors either. Instead, when someone sins against us, the best thing we can do for others is acknowledge the full extent of their sin and completely forgive them based on Jesus' love expressed on the cross. That may take time. It's okay to be patient with ourselves and anyone else affected by sin.

When we refuse to accept responsibility for our own sin, we reject God's offer of His mercy and grace. Yet, we daily need mercy and grace for ongoing sinful attitudes and habits. We may accept His offer of forgiveness and salvation, but still get stuck in unhealthy attitudes and habits. His forgiveness is for all our sins, past, present, and future. Accepting His forgiveness begins the process of getting free of selfish attitudes. Healthy habits follow on the heels of healthy attitudes.

In the example of my dad's amends, he acknowledged the emotional abandonment we both experienced. He could have easily denied his own culpability, even though he was the parent in the relationship. He could have blamed his childhood or ignored the way his pain hobbled him, thus affecting me. Instead, my courageous, humble dad owned his part of our experience. He received forgiveness from God and asked for my forgiveness for covering his pain with alcohol instead of dealing with it sooner. He freed himself and me simultaneously. Plus, he created a tender moment of fellowship between us. What a powerful example of taking ownership of wounded attitudes and habits, even denial!

The Danger of Pretensions

The Bible addresses this problem of self-deception or denial in 1 John 1:8–10 "If we say that we have no sin, we deceive ourselves, and the truth is not in us. If we confess our sins, He is faithful and just to forgive us *our* sins and to cleanse us from all unrighteousness. If we say that we have not sinned, we make Him a liar, and His word is not in us." The danger in denial is thinking we can somehow perfect ourselves. Self-perfection smacks of self-righteousness.

God's salvation is complete. His forgiveness for any recurring sin is available on the spot as we turn to Him for help and freedom. Will sinful attitudes and habits make us and everyone around us miserable? Yep, probably so. It is serious business when a Christian lives a lifestyle denying God's power. We should tremble and pray for ourselves and others. Basically, denial is pretending we're perfect. Pretensions are silly. We may fool ourselves, but we're not fooling anybody else. Just ask a toddler what Mommy did that was naughty. Grandparents often hear all the nitty-gritty details of the parents' mistakes whenever grandchildren come over to visit. Some of their reports are pretty funny, but surprisingly accurate!

All humans are tempted to lie to ourselves. For some reason, we all seem to need to prove how perfect we are. If it weren't so dangerous, such pretensions would be funny. Perfect? Really?

Besides, when we pretend to be perfect, we tend to do weird things to keep up our image. Denial often shows up in three varieties of symptoms: blaming others, making excuses, and playing the victim card. They are basically rooted in the same need to deny our culpability.

We've all been tempted to blame others for our mistakes. When we blame others, we turn over the responsibility for our decisions to them. We may blame God for our frailties by claiming He made us with a tendency to be selfish in certain areas. "God made me this way. I can't help it."

The same thinking prompts us to make excuses when we mess up. When we make excuses, what we're saying is, "I'm normally perfect, and I would be this time, except for these uncontrollable circumstances. It's not my fault; it's the circumstances."

When we play the victim card, we communicate we are not responsible for our own decisions. We believe we are somehow helpless, unable to make changes even with the help of God. We may believe our issues are so big or so awful they don't warrant God's grace and help.

When we blame others, make excuses, or play the victim card, we act like we ourselves don't need forgiveness. Once we quit pretending to be perfect, we can relax and experience the forgiveness all around us, put in place by a God who loves us.

In another manifestation of denial, as modern Christians we sometimes do penance. For instance, we may wring our hands and confess our sins from years ago over and over. In an effort to clear our conscience, we may do things to assuage our guilt. When we do penance, we are saying Jesus' work on the cross covers many sins, but not my particularly awful ones.

An example of this might be a post-abortive woman who volunteers at a pregnancy center because she still carries around guilt from her abortion. There's nothing inherently wrong with volunteering, but trying to wash our conscious by volunteering won't work. Only Jesus' blood works that particular kind of pure cleansing power.

Contagious Compassion

By being so honest, Dad freed himself to focus on my hurt. He was able to listen honestly and compassionately to me because his heart was ready to take the full impact of how his old pain burdened me. Compassion is like communicable disease, passing from person to person, but in a good way!

God starts the transmission of compassion. God wholeheartedly wants people to come to Him in a tender, loving relationship. Jesus predicted His own death, with God's desire in mind, saying, "And I, if I am lifted up from the earth, will draw all *peoples* to Myself" (John 12:32). If we believe God can't handle our issues, we misrepresent His true nature. He is the mighty God who rules heaven and earth. He certainly is able to handle our sin.

Our problem of sin was settled long before you or I arrived on this earth. All we are required to do is acknowledge our need for His forgiveness, which He prepared for us in advance by way of the cross. When we acknowledge our own sin and His mercy, we lift Him up in order to draw others to Him.

Denial means we refuse to listen to the gentle voice of His Holy Spirit whispering, "Trust Me." Forgiveness is a prepaid package deal.

Unforgiveness, such a destructive factor in marriage or any relationship, often tanks communication. I don't like playing around with such a dangerous habit as denial. Each day, I try my best to be squared away when I need to ask forgiveness of anyone. Forgiveness has an added bonus. It frees us to listen with compassion. We've been forgiven. Now we have compassion to pass on to others.

Amazingly, when we own up to our failures and pain, we often find the other person prepared to forgive us and welcome us freely. Not always, but sometimes it's that simple. What an amazing way to experience freedom and unconditional love! Compassion and forgiveness spread faster in families than a toddler's contagious cold and are a lot more fun to catch.

When we hold grudges rather than forgiving our spouses, our minds begin to play tricks on us. We begin to believe we never sinned, at least not in this case, we think. Such foolish thinking infects our hearts, making honest listening nearly impossible.

Integrity begins with getting the hard stuff out of the way, especially self-forgiveness. Practicing forgiveness frees us to experience life and all its adventure, including intimate conversation. Integrity means forgiving in the most difficult places, especially forgiving our own self-inflicted pain. Phew. Drawing so deeply is hard work. Fortunately, forgiveness often rewards us with incentives for our effort, like the tender story Dad added to my collection that day. What a cherished memory with my beloved dad!

The Comfort We Share

When we share our broken heart honestly, once healed, we listen strategically to others with humility. How? Because we know firsthand the power in forgiveness.

Paul explains comfort and compassion this way in his second letter to the Corinthians: "Blessed *be* the God and Father of our Lord Jesus Christ, the Father of mercies and God of all comfort, who comforts us in all our tribulation, that we may be able to comfort those who are in any trouble, with the comfort with which we ourselves are comforted by God. For as the sufferings of Christ abound in us, so our consolation also abounds through Christ" (2 Corinthians 1:3–5).

Our relationships prosper when we listen strategically with heartfelt compassion. By strategic listening, I mean we can listen with an ear for the things a husband or friends may truly and deeply need. This kind of integrity allows us to look into others' hearts, offering an intimate kind of comfort. Sometimes, we see what our husband needs before he does.

Such intimacy only comes with hard work and years of practicing integrity in our deepest places. Forgiveness rewards us with rich understanding. We begin to cherish each other more freely and habitually. We experience a deep walk with God, listening and hearing the whisper of His Spirit. He becomes the gentle companion of our soul. Courage to be truthful with your own heart initiates a new level of vulnerability with your husband. If your heart embraces such courage, please know how proud I am of you.

In Case You Were Wondering...

How do I forgive myself? Oh my. This is a hard one. We all seem to struggle with self-forgiveness even as we trust the cross. I know countless women, including myself, who have momentarily conquered the obstacle, only to have unforgiveness pop up again. We sometimes cling to self-righteousness because we are afraid to admit our own sinfulness.

The temptation can be subtle. Our subconscious often tries to tell us when we need to forgive ourselves. If you do penance or hide your problem, pay attention. Sometimes this sounds like self-rejection in our thoughts. Or we may review how bad our mistakes were over and over, like a saint in the Middle Ages dragging around a heavy wooden cross. Subconsciously, we may believe by reviewing our sins, our penance will somehow make amends to God for our failures.

Imagine forgiveness like a sixteen-year-old who receives the gift of a shiny new car from his parents but goes to the dealership each month and tries to keep making car payments anyway. How ridiculous! Who would do such a thing? Imagine how annoyed his parents would be if he kept insisting he had to pay for the car they already paid for.

Have no doubt, Jesus completely paid the price for our sin once and for all. We have no need to do penance. Instead, like a sixteen-year-old with a new car, we can accept the gift with joy!

Jesus' resurrection proves His authority over sin and death. We receive His gift freely offered by simply accepting it from Him. We're saved by His grace, not our misguided efforts at perfection and pretensions.

Pause, Ponder, Pray, and then Proceed

Forgiveness is a powerful force of nature. Yet, the hardest person to forgive is often ourselves. Self-forgiveness releases compassion for others. Compassionate listening follows closely on the footsteps of forgiveness.

1. Understanding your needs: In a safe place, write down any bitter thoughts currently circling in your head. Ask God to help you forgive anyone who causes bitterness to flow from your heart. Now write positive prayers and truths across from each one. This is not an easy exercise, but a healthy one.

Here's a perfect example from many victorious women I know. Negative, self-condemning thought: I'm mad at myself for waiting so long to get my mammogram. Prayer: Help me forgive myself, Lord, since You forgave me already. Positive, God-focused thought: Thank You, Lord, for surrounding me with women and health professionals who have walked the path of breast cancer before me. "And He said to me, 'My grace is sufficient for you, for My strength is made perfect in weakness.' Therefore most gladly I will rather boast in my infirmities, that the power of Christ may rest upon me" (2 Corinthians 12:9).

2. Identifying your worth: In those deep places where you feel you don't deserve good things, how does your thinking need to change so you can humbly and victoriously forgive yourself? Please pay attention in your list for anything smacking of penance or self-punishment. Jesus' cross covers self-condemnation.

3. Envisioning your future: When you are free of the penance of negative self-talk, what can you do with the energy you save? Does your husband need to process a difficult, lingering hurt at some point soon? Ask God to give you special insight when it comes to binding up the broken heart of your husband.

163

My prayer for you, with my love

Dear God, the One who listens with tender compassion, hear now our deepest sorrows. All women battle condemnation. We feel condemned and are tempted to condemn others. In our dark moments we need to be filled with light. We all need to experience Your forgiveness. Whether my sister needs to forgive herself or someone else, I pray You help her begin to move past this serious challenge. Empower her to forgive anyone who has injured her, Your beloved daughter. Strengthen her, O Lord!

Please bless her with the confidence that You alone can forgive her. You do forgive her now, as she looks to You. Please surprise her with the sparkling light of forgiveness. Oh, the glorious freedom of Your forgiveness!

Together, from Psalm 18:28–29, we claim the light You alone are able to offer: "For you will light my lamp; the LORD my God will enlighten my darkness. For by You I can run against a troop, by You I can leap over a wall."

To pray for yourself

Forgive me, Good Father. Strengthen me to forgive myself. Let me reflect the powerful cleansing available because of the blood of Your Son. Cleanse me of all residual guilt and shame from past experiences by Your Son's powerful blood. Release me from condemnation, especially self-condemnation. Teach me to walk in forgiveness moment by moment. Help me to strengthen my husband in healing, hope, and joy. Bless me now because that's Your heart's desire. In Jesus' name I pray. Amen.

"It is in pardoning that we are pardoned." —**Francis of Assisi**

CHAPTER FOURTEEN

Negotiate Like an Oil Tycoon

How do we negotiate well so basic needs and wants get met in our marriage?

By recognizing that when God is in the process everyone gets a blessing.

Arguing and blaming each other for close to an hour, as usual, we spent hard-earned cash to go nowhere fast. Then, in a split second, our counselor asked a pivotal question.

"Cathy, what do you want?"

I hemmed and hawed for a minute, offering some vague suggestions like I wanted David to be nice to me or I wanted help with the home-schooling. Then, a lightbulb blinked on momentarily, and I told the brilliant truth.

"Honestly, I don't know. I can tell you what everyone else in my family needs and wants, but I have no idea what I need," I admitted sheepishly. Then, gathering my courage I added a pledge I faithfully keep to this day. "Tell ya what, I will think about it and next month I will come back with a list of things I want and need."

My list—thirty items long and growing—astonished me by the time we met the next month. Once I finally sat down to write it, my thoughts burst through my brain fog like soldiers ready for battle in orderly lines appearing on paper as fast as I could write them. Done in minutes, I popped my list into the green binder where I kept all my personal diagnoses about how our marriage needed serious work and prayer. My green binder recorded the emotional medical history of a marriage that was in cardiac arrest.

My biggest desire was for my marriage to meet some of the emotional needs going unmet in my life. I wasn't unrealistic enough to think one person could meet all my needs. But I was worn out.

I regularly recharged David's emotional energy. I made intentional decisions to listen to him and offer encouragement. Our family calls the process debriefing the day. But it seemed my own emotional energy stayed depleted. Primarily, I needed his heart to be tender towards me in ways he found challenging.

Our quest to negotiate for a better marriage pursued two end results. Number one: to get more of our needs met by learning to be specific about what we needed. Number two: to get some of our wants met by learning to cherish each other with better understanding. The secret is to know what you want and need. For women, knowing what you want and need can be especially tricky.

I came to our next counseling meeting armed and dangerous. Nothing freaks out a husband quite as much as a wife who knows what she wants, especially if he's not used to what he may perceive as demands.

David found it pretty sexy, it turns out. Plus, there was more good news. When I started remembering the girl David married, it occurred to me he hadn't married a wimp. That brave, bold girl lost herself under the weight of caring so much about all the people I love. It was time to take a breath, come up for air, and take care of me before our marriage imploded.

Let's Make a Good Deal

To this day, David negotiates better than I do. With years of experience in the oil business, he knows how to make a deal. I'm not exactly a pushover, but I get distracted. On one hand, when I'm having fun, I tend to forget important issues. David, on the other hand, doggedly sticks to his goals and brings other people along in the process, especially me.

For example, I'm as happy as a small child with a lollipop to drive into work together in the mornings. However, we may stop for several of his errands before I realize I'm losing valuable writing time at the office. Lost time doesn't have to be a big problem, if I can just remember to clarify my day's schedule with David. Once I share my priorities for the day, he is happy to work together toward our mutual goals.

It took me years to figure out I habitually let my own daily goals slide in favor of his. His priorities were getting accomplished each day, but mine were not. I resented the lost time until I learned to negotiate better with clear communication about my needs and wants for the day.

Finding a way to negotiate where we both felt like co-winners emerged as a worthy goal for us both. By expressing my needs and wants clearly, I empowered us to get there together. For those moments when we simply don't agree, negotiating clearly solves a lot of potential problems. Years ago, a friend told me that marriage was one long conversation. Being a natural communicator, I like that idea.

But I gotta tell ya, I've learned marriage is one long negotiation, too. I don't want you to wimp out and end up mad and hurt like I did. Instead, you can come away from negotiations feeling like you are a winner and queen of your family. Negotiating well means all people feel satisfied, providing harmony in marriage.

I understand many women live with a man who refuses to negotiate. It's his way or nothing. Yet, part of negotiating means bringing people to the table with a deal they want to make. Acquiring some negotiating skills does you both a favor, even if he doesn't know he needs help.

Negotiating is a serious communication skill set. I've given serious thought to how we negotiate a marriage that's a blessing to all. By all, I mean the husband, the wife, the kids, and all the extended family. Let's face it, a problematic marriage makes everyone uncomfortable, even friends, neighbors, and complete strangers.

A wife whose needs and wants go unmet for a long time will struggle with resentment. Eventually, resentment and discouragement will surface in the marriage as distress and bitterness.

Five Tips to Get a Great Deal

For some reason I don't understand, men often read distress as crazy, like the wife is out of control. Perhaps, denial is more comfortable for the husband than recognizing his responsibility to be an initiating leader. A man's heart can get hard quickly if he can blame his wife for being crazy, rather than admit he is failing at marriage. We know divorce is rooted in hard heartedness.

Learning to negotiate like an oil tycoon means your marriage has a better chance of survival. Solving ongoing problems through excellent negotiation releases the tension and stress placed on marriage by unmet needs and wants. Good negotiations result in happier marriages, blessing lots of folks around us.

In order to negotiate well, we must nail down four basic ingredients, then evaluate our deal based on a fifth principle. Here are the secrets to negotiating like an oil tycoon.

Respecting Mutual Giftedness

First, we must respect each person's giftedness, including our own. I pity the oil deal made with only geologists on the team, for instance. Geologists bring their unique talents to a project, but they depend on others like engineers, too. In the same way, couples rely on each other's giftedness to thrive.

Women particularly get so busy serving our families, we forget our own identity. This may also be true for men. If you forget your own dreams, priorities, or heck even your own personality, you may spend a lot of time chasing things that don't matter to you. Ask yourself this, "Who am I and what do I bring to the marriage?"

Remembering our identity includes remembering our own inadequacies. There are skills and gifts I won't live long enough to acquire. Respecting what your husband brings to the table helps you appreciate each other.

For instance, when David and I sit down with the budget together each quarter, I depend on him to understand the numbers better than

I do. While David is better at math, I'm natural at timely habits. I'm the one who prods him to sit down regularly, even when he's groaning about spending a Saturday morning working on the budget. Once we finish the process, we're both grateful for each other's skill set. By the way, budgets are a fine communication tool for negotiating together to figure out mutual priorities.

I can laugh about negotiating like an oil tycoon, but in the energy business, collaboration depends on good negotiations. Every project requires investors, geologists, engineers, and field hands to respect each other and work together. Anyone who can't express succinctly what they need or want on a drilling rig puts everyone else in danger. Lives can be at risk in such a dangerous work environment if anyone fails to communicate their needs.

Understanding what each member brings to the team creates an environment rich in gratitude and collaboration. Gratitude is a wonderful way to cherish each other.

Name the Desired Outcome

Second, we must figure out what we want. An energy executive would never consider making a deal without naming the desired outcome. All goals are specifically spelled out. Oil wells, for instance, can cost millions of dollars to drill. Without proper planning, a failed well can mean bankruptcy. Bankruptcy affects all vendors down the line. Therefore, each negotiation begins with a prospectus and business plan with clearly defined outcomes.

To negotiate like an oil tycoon, you have to trust your work partners to do what is right for everyone involved. In negotiating with your husband, if he fails to appreciate and honor you, you may need to negotiate for more respect immediately.

We can't negotiate for what we want if we don't know what we need. Defining our dreams allows us to examine them realistically. Even far-fetched dreams can become a reality when we tie them down, divide them in chunks, and cover them in prayer. Our purpose statement and personal etiquette will help us identify the type of mutual respect and vision for the future we want to build into our marriage.

We can begin to raise the standard on our own behavior without saying a word about it to our husband. We must begin by respecting ourselves no matter what else we may need or want in a marriage. Behaving respectfully toward myself and others became a powerful communication tool to negotiate well in my home.

I like what Peter says about raising the bar on respect in a home, "Wives, likewise, *be* submissive to your own husbands, that even if some do not obey the word, they, without a word, may be won by the conduct of their wives, when they observe your chaste conduct accompanied by fear [your respect of God]" (1 Peter 3:1–2).

Sometimes women trip over the idea of submitting to their husbands. The idea of submission here is to devote ourselves to the best interests of our husband. Isn't that our natural tendency? I believe Peter knew a woman's natural tendency to devotion. Women put everyone else first, it seems, as natural care givers. I put David's priorities ahead of my own naturally.

The trick is to negotiate for my priorities, so we're both happy in the long run. I do us both a favor by respecting myself and labeling my needs and wants. It is certainly in a husband's best interests to have a happy wife. A wise husband will want to know what inspires his wife.

The word fear in Peter's wisdom can be confusing. He's not telling us to be afraid of our husbands. Far from it, he's commanding us to be courageous and full of confidence as we respect God. It's so much easier to treat others respectfully when we respect ourselves, knowing God cares for us.

Chaste conduct sounds like an old-fashioned term, but it simply means to behave in a respectful way toward ourselves and others. A chaste attitude at home reminds me of the guy at work who quits cussing when he realizes the rest of the team isn't using profanity. Chaste conduct has a way of setting a high bar of respect, without saying a word.

Other times we do need to speak up, though. Remember we are joining God in His creative process. God created the world by speaking it into existence. Speaking the truth gently, even assertively, can help promote the right direction in our marriage, especially when we've spelled out what we hope to accomplish. Once He spoke the earth into existence, God declared it good! We can learn from the good Father's example.

Know a Good Deal for Your Partner

Third, you must listen for what your spouse wants. Like a businessman presenting an oil prospect to a potential partner, we must understand the other person's needs and wants. The deal needs to be good for everyone or business partners won't buy in. In the same way, negotiations in marriage must take into account both spouses' needs and wants. If a spouse is not content, bitterness may creep in.

"One reason some people have stable marriages may be that they are good at listening past the edge in their partner's voice to the positive or conciliatory message behind it," writes author John Gottman. In contrast, he adds, "Like a car stuck in the mud, they (some couples) frantically spin their wheels but get nowhere. What makes this especially tragic is that both partners probably can problem solve well when confronted with difficulty not related to their marriage."[33]

Gottman's description perfectly described my marriage communication issues with David. I found myself spinning my wheels with my own husband. As a communication expert, the process of trying and failing to communicate drove me crazy.

We don't want our own needs and wants to go unaddressed. Neither do we want to sabotage our husband's contentment by dominating the negotiations. No one wants to feel slammed or shut down by one's spouse.

Still, we may not like the initial results when we first try to negotiate with a new perspective. When our efforts seem to fail frequently, it's easy to become bitter.

Gratitude is the antidote for bitterness. However, it's hard to be grateful if we don't know what we want. I learned thanking God for my husband's positive traits—the ones I found attractive from the begin-

---

33 John Gottman, *Why Marriages Succeed or Fail...and How You Can Make Yours Last* (New York: Simon Schuster Paperbacks, 1994), 100.

ning—gave me a reason to simmer down. Soon, I could proceed more judiciously in my effort to negotiate for what I needed and wanted.

Additionally, listening for the dreams and desires of your husband sets him up to be grateful for you. You can help him vocalize his dreams. Once he has words for what he needs and wants, he may be more grateful to you when he realizes you naturally seek to help him. In turn, he may be more open to listening for your dreams as you learn to vocalize them.

We can't meet all of each other's needs and wants. But we can agree to tick off some items on our lists together. Praying together for shared dreams allows you both to thank God as He answers. If your husband is reluctant to participate in the process of negotiating for a better marriage, find positive ways to vocalize your needs and wants anyway.

God is in the Process

Fourth, we must keep watch for the things God intends for our marriage. We ask a husband for what we need and want, but we ask God also. Often, our prayers include help in finding new options to bless both spouses. God grants us creativity in negotiating for the best ways to bless our marriage.

It might surprise folks to know how often people in the oil business pray. I know Hollywood likes to make oil companies the bad guys. But in real life, people in the energy industry are hard-working middle-class folks in an extremely volatile business who trust God. I've seen it often. The same rough field hands who are cussing one minute are asking for prayer the next. In a business fraught with risk and danger, people can experience crisis on any given day. Those who own small businesses in the energy industry learn quickly to trust God or get out of the business.

In the same way, marriage is risky business. We trust God for the best, knowing at any moment a crisis may develop. One perfect example as I write, my husband has been through two knee replacement surgeries this year. While we traveled through health challenges, our better communication skills have sure been tested. Thank goodness, we did the work years ago. All marriages adjust to change along the way, whether it's a new baby, an independent teenager, the price of college, or aging knees. Watching for God along the way smooths out the rough spots a bit and strengthens us.

If we skip the step of watching for God's blessings, we may miss out on fulfilling His impossible dream for us. A purpose statement sure comes in handy if we want to know how well our marriage is fulfilling its purpose in our lives. Who cares if everyone else views our purpose statement as unrealistic? While others waste time criticizing our idealism, we might actually fulfill the mighty work God planned for us as a couple.

Good marriages, like the energy business, run on great negotiations. To be successful, an oil tycoon respects what each person brings to the team, knows exactly what they hope to accomplish, understands what all partners need and want, and looks to God to bless the process for everyone. To sum up the four key ingredients of good negotiations for marriage, we must know what we bring to the marriage, know what we need and want, listen well to understand the needs and wants of our spouse, and ask God for options to bless both spouses.

Everyone Gets a Blessing!

Finally, when you've negotiated for something new in your relationship, evaluate the results this way—make no mistake: When God is in the process, everyone gets a blessing!

I like what John Gottman says on the topic of happy marriages, "Happy couples are not so very different from unhappy couples; they are simply able to make repairs to their relationship easier and faster so they can get back to the joy of being together."[34] Negotiating a blessing for everyone as you make small changes in the right direction will inevitably lead to more energy for cherishing each other.

Negotiations stall if one person is habitually satisfied while the other spouse chafes. If one person gets the short stick regularly, the mar-

---

34 John Gottman, *Eight Dates: Essential Conversations for a Lifetime of Love* (New York: Workman Publishing Company), Kindle Edition.

riage's foundation will suffer. Consistently winning can turn out to be a net loss when it comes to marriage. Both spouses should consistently feel like winners. In a strong marriage, everyone feels consistently blessed and grateful. Productive negotiations communicate a wealth of delight in the relationship.

In many ways, marriage is the hardest negotiation because the relationship is so intimate. Albert Einstein said, "Men marry women with the hope they will never change. Women marry men with the hope they will change. Invariably they are both disappointed."[35]

Negotiating for the freedom to be imperfect is a mutual blessing. We often get help from each other where we need it when we can trust each other to love unconditionally.

A couple of other great things happen when we learn to make deals where everyone feels like a winner. We prepare ourselves to succeed in negotiations anywhere else. Plus, we set a terrific example for our children to follow throughout their lives. Learning to look to God for a blessing for everyone may seem like a small change, but it results in terrific dividends.

In Case You Were Wondering...

How do I keep from feeling taken for granted? Brag about yourself. Yes, I said it. I know it feels weird, but just do it. Tell everyone in your family that you are the awesome queen of everything you see. If they don't believe you, banish them from your kingdom, especially at dinnertime. Trust me, they will come around to the correct perspective. Okay, maybe that's a little extreme. Although, it has been known to happen at my house.

For the woman who has a naturally gentle disposition, man, I wish I had your gift! I've seen good women bring their husband and family into order, restoring kind attitudes with a gentle appeal to their consciences.

No matter your personality, there are times when we all have to remind our families how lucky they are to have us. When I do it humbly

---

35 Albert Einstein, http://www.goodreads.com/quotes/41411-men-marry-women-with-the-hope-they-will-never-change, 11-02-16

as a request for appreciation, it works well. Gratitude is a huge blessing, so it's okay to ask your family to dish up some gratitude for you!

Seriously, learning to negotiate for what you need before your boundaries are trampled is a crucial skill set in marriage. Good negotiations create blessings for everyone in the family. Yet, there are common habits that prevent true negotiations and produce arguments. How do we easily transform any argument back into a conversation? All you have to do is ask a good question. I'm not kidding. It's that easy. Keep reading for more about power questions in chapter 15. Voila!

Pause, Ponder, Pray, and then Proceed

When we understand the five tips to negotiating well, we are much more likely to get what we need and want from our marriage. Since we are seeking a healthy marriage, we look for blessings for both spouses. Soon we habitually anticipate deals everyone loves!

1. Understanding your needs: What if you treated your instincts like your best friends and listened to them, what would they tell you? What are the top five things you wish were true in your marriage? Write down five needs or wants you wish you could say were met in your marriage. God wants to bless you. What small change could you make today to yield dividends later?

2. Identifying your worth: What recent comment about you reminds you about all the good stuff you offer? It is so important to feel confident about what you bring to your marriage. What do your dreams tell you about the plans God has for you? Your dreams probably consist of your needs and wants. God is moving in your heart to help you identify His plans for you. What is His Holy Spirit whispering? Speak that whisper out loud to a trusted friend.

3. Envisioning your future: What could you do this week to take better care of yourself? What breakthrough victory in your marriage would make you feel like a co-winner? What fun and refreshing thing did you do this week? Make plans now to do something to cherish yourself today.

My prayer for you, with my love

Dear God, please bless my sister with the marriage of her dreams. When we all feel taken advantage of in our marriages, it's so easy for us to despair, Lord. Feeling victimized, our love easily turns to wrath, almost before we know it. Help her know who she is and what she needs and wants. We beg You for Your help, so she victoriously negotiates well for the sake of all those who love her. She wants a deal that honors You. Honestly, she just wants a deal that lets her be the queen of her family. She wants to be a co-winner in all her marital negotiations. Fortunately, that's what You want for her. Jesus, You are the One named as her Advocate. We trust You.

Together we rejoice in You with the words from Psalm 18:30, "*As for God, His way is perfect; The word of the* LORD *is proven; He is a shield to all who trust in Him.*"

To pray for yourself

Good Father, You are the One who loves me with unfailing love. You give me hope when despair threatens to swallow me up. Victimhood is not my only option. You prove victorious for me. You extend mercy to my heart when I feel wrathful. Your plans unfold as I seek a deepening relationship with You. Wrap me in Your arms and strengthen me to negotiate well and even stand alone when necessary. Remind me I am actually never alone. Teach me to be assertive and clear, perhaps the best gift I give my husband. Hold my head up in dignity. What I truly want is unity with You, the Lover of my soul and spirit. Direct me in the path You have for me, unique and wonderful me. Give me patience as I tread Your path for my marriage. Bless me now because that's Your heart's desire. In Jesus' name I pray. Amen.

"Let us never negotiate out of fear. But let us never fear to negotiate."
—**John Fitzgerald Kennedy**, from his Inaugural Address, January 20, 1961.

CHAPTER FIFTEEN

Power Questions

How do we change an argument into a conversation?

By asking gentle questions.

my dad once asked Meme if she had a parachute left over from WWII. Dad needed a parachute for the perfect party decoration. Yep, Meme had a parachute, as a matter of fact. One never knows when one might need a silk parachute with holes in it. She went to a spare bedroom closet stuffed with similarly useful necessities and came back as victorious as if she had single-handedly beaten the Nazis herself.

Hoarding crept up on me stealthily. When exactly did I begin to hoard questions? Who knows? Without realizing it, I started collecting questions, and now I can't stop. For instance, I wrote the first chapter for this book, and when I came back to it a few days later, I realized it was pages and pages of questions. My first editor, the amazing Sandra Beck, made me answer all the dang things. When I finally finished answering them all, I held a completed manuscript! Then she limited me to only three in a row. After years of interviewing, writing, and podcasting, questions tumble out on any topic, like the treasures in Meme's closets.

Just like all serious hoarders, knowing the value of a good question, I keep tons of them around. You know, in case anyone else ever needs them. The right question can change the world. If world peace was one question away, I probably have the exact question. Certainly, a good question can change our marriages and bring peace. Asking a good question is the fastest way to reestablish oneness with your husband. In fact, the way to change an argument back into a conversation simply involves asking the right question.

Miracle-working Power Questions

If you can imagine a world with conversation instead of arguments, then I have tremendous news for you. A powerful question works miracles! I'm not talking about snarky, sarcastic questions, although I've worn out my own stockpile of those. The best way to authentic conversations instead of arguments with your hubby is to ask a gentle question. There's so much power in gentleness.

If you two argue a lot, you may be filled with doubts about your husband's love. Believe me, I understand. David and I are both analytical people. That creates some intense, um, let's say discussions, when we disagree. You may need to find a professional counselor to help you understand whether your arguments are healthy discourse or something more sinister, like control issues. I was relieved when we discovered the power of a gentle question. I hope the small change to gentle questions puts power for peace in your hands as well.

If discussions at your house feel too intense, please try a different approach. Who knows? Maybe your husband finds you so mysterious he can't figure out what to ask you. Start by trading fun questions you will both enjoy. What is your favorite thing about your best friend? Where did you learn to be so good at organizing volunteer events? What is your happiest childhood memory?

Remarkably, questions ignite transformative power. Jesus said it this way: "Ask, and it will be given to you; seek, and you will find; knock, and it will be opened to you. *For everyone who asks receives,* and he who seeks finds, and to him who knocks it will be opened" (Matthew 7:7–8 emphasis mine). Ask, seek, knock. The process of gaining wisdom begins with questions. To get you started, below are a few I particularly like. (But I'm always adding to my collection, so feel free to send me your favorites!)

- What do *you* want to happen out of this? Or another way: What would be the best outcome of this conversation from your point of view? I use this at the beginning of all meetings. I just put it right on the agenda. When you use this question, you're letting the other person know they can trust you to care about them.

- When we have these tough conversations, how could I make it better? This question holds *both* people responsible for noticing when things get out of hand. When you use this one at home, you are training your family that conversation is a two-way street.

- Would it help you to know what makes me feel uncomfortable? He may say no. But, if your husband says yes, you have his permission to talk about feelings.

- What you're sayin' is…? Then, you repeat back what they just said to be sure you understood. Or, am I understanding you correctly if I say this? This one's a classic. It works. One thing I like about this question is both people have a responsibility to speak up and to listen. Both.

- What do *you* wish I would ask? Or, is there more I should know here? There are many variations to this question. I try to ask one of these at the end of every interview. I call my favorite one the megaphone question: If you had a megaphone and could shout anything, what would you shout?

- What is your favorite thing about me especially when we don't agree? This is my personal favorite. I'm always surprised when David answers it.

Notice how many of those questions focus on the other person. Yet, a couple encourage him to think of your needs. Pure genius and great negotiations require us to ask good questions, alert for ways *everyone* can receive a blessing.

For example, before we can cherish each other in our marriages, we must ask ourselves how cherishing looks to us. Often women reverse the logical order and put others' opinions before their own. Initially, we may tend to ask gentle questions of our husbands. But, before long, we must ask ourselves the same tender questions about what we want in a marriage.

Best Outcomes

Normally, if a husband gets push back from his wife in arguments, then it may take him a while to realize a change needs to emerge. Push back tends to put people on the defensive. Instead of telling him how the cow ate the cabbage, ask him gently about what he wants. *What would be the best outcome in this conversation for you, dear?*

He may suspect your motives or try to second-guess your questions. He might fail to answer until he figures out he actually wants to answer. Imagine his surprise when he realizes you asked because you want to know what he considers a good deal for himself.

What's even more fascinating for wives is the way Jesus offered context in the earlier verses. Right before instructing us to ask, seek, knock, He says this, "Do not give what is holy to the dogs; nor cast your pearls before swine, lest they trample them under their feet, and turn and tear you in pieces" (Matthew 7:6). Not that our husbands are swine. But, oh my, how often I've given my husband the full extent of my spirituality without ever letting him get a word in edgewise. No wonder I like questions—they release me from my duties as the family know-it-all!

Being too quick to share an opinion can get us all in trouble sometimes. We may even get labeled as judgmental. Look at the verses immediately preceding for the low-down on what Jesus says about being judgmental: "Judge not, that you be not judged. For with what judgment you judge, you will be judged; and with the measure you use, it will be measured back to you" (Matthew 7:1–2).

In other words, the judgmental assumptions we dish out bounce back to splatter on us. We are wise when we ask questions instead of assuming we know already. The next verses give us some great advice about how to mind our own business.

"And why do you look at the speck in your brother's eye, but do not consider the plank in your own eye? Or how can you say to your brother, 'Let me remove the speck from your eye'; and look, a plank is in your own eye? Hypocrite! First remove the plank from your own eye, and then you will see clearly to remove the speck from your brother's eye" (Matthew 7:3–5).

Especially when it comes to the heart of a husband, we don't have to judge. We can trust the forces God set loose in the universe. For instance, consequences balance free will, creating goodness in life. While it may sound tough, trusting God is so much easier than fulfilling my role as self-appointed judge and jury. Plus, I keep getting distracted with all these planks in my own eye.

Why Not Ask?

Maybe you have questions you always wanted answered. In the midst of a brilliant treatise on how we have victory over temptation, James dropped this little pearl, addressing the question of asking: "You fight and war. Yet you do not have because you do not ask" (James 4:2). Wow!

But what is James instructing us to ask for? "But the wisdom that is from above is first pure, then peaceable, gentle, willing to yield, full of mercy and good fruits, without partiality and without hypocrisy. Now the fruit of righteousness is sown in peace by those who make peace" (James 3:17–18). Okay, now James is just stepping all over my toes!

Still, we want peace in our marriages and homes. Are we willing to fight for peace? James uses words like, "pure, then peaceable, gentle, willing to yield, full of mercy and good fruits, without partiality and without hypocrisy" to describe the kind of wisdom we want. My, my. Those words are easy to read and hard to live by!

Only if we redefine what it means to hang tough, will we succeed in the battle for healthy marriage conversations. We must fight with wisdom; to get real peace with joy takes wisdom. Like wise soldiers in real battle, we don't charge the enemy like a bunch of crazy, self-destructive fools. Besides, why would we treat those we love like the enemy?

Instead, we plan our battle strategy judiciously, praying for no casualties. When marriage seems more like a battleground than a joint venture, we don't have to avoid confrontation. Instead, we can promote peace by handling conflict gently and judiciously. Asking wise questions and listening provides an excellent battle plan for restoring peace in marriage.

I don't think it's any accident all this information includes a scathing comment: "the tongue *is* a fire, a world of iniquity" (James 3:6). Personally, whenever I open the book of James, I feel I would be safer if I kept a fire extinguisher handy. My own tongue has sparked many a fire.

Peace at Home, No Assumptions

We want to ask gentle questions. Naturally, we want our husbands to behave gently, mercifully, judiciously, and kindly. Wouldn't it be wonderful if those same adjectives described us? We all crave peace in our homes, but how do you ask for peace when tempers are flaring like bombs bursting in air on the Fourth of July?

For the sake of peace, we start with one gentle, insightful question at a time. Surprisingly, we may instantly receive true, tender insight into a husband's heart. With good questions, we begin to collect information about how we can serve our husband effectively. We may even hoard this information, if you will, like the invaluable, random stuff my Meme collected in her closets.

Rather than assuming, guessing, getting it wrong, and hurting his feelings in ways he can't even communicate, we can begin to savor truth about his heart. Not demanding to be served, instead, we can serve by asking for clear information. With the first gentle question, we are transforming a habit of arguing into a new way of cherishing each other. Just a gentle question or two about what it would look like if….

With a gentle question, we transform arguments into conversations and negotiate for a lasting peace on the home front.

In Case You Were Wondering...

We argue a lot, so how do I deal with general anxiety? Depression? When arguing is a habitual process in our homes, most women feel anxious. We may feel depressed when we assume we are helpless to change our circumstances. I'm not a counselor or therapist, so I can only speak from my own experience with anxiety and depression.

First of all, your anxiety may just be a byproduct of the fact that you are a conscientious, administrative, peace-making person. If this is you, please sit by me.

Second, anxiety and depression may signal what God wants to accomplish next in our lives. God may be speaking to you through uncomfortable emotions He designed to inform us.

Next, some of our anxiety and depression may stem from feeling we don't have a voice in our own home. With small changes, you can advocate for yourself.

Also, since anxiety and depression are real, please consider some medical advice. Your brain is part of your body, and it may need a little professional TLC. Don't forget to ask your doctor about hormones. Blah. Hormones can be so annoying.

As women, we all get worn out. Issues pile up, causing anxiety and depression. Daily life can start to short-circuit us like a low-grade fever knocks out a toddler. Boom! We've all been there. Instead, with a good friend or counselor create a strategy for change, including some gentle power questions.

Questions are bright and sparkly every time you share one with a friend. In fact, sharing questions makes them more wonderful. Please send me your questions. I'm a hoarder, ahem, I meant to say, collector.

Pause, Ponder, Pray, and then Proceed

The transforming power of a gentle question emboldens us so much we want to keep a bunch of good questions available at a moment's notice. Transforming an argument with your hubby back into a conversation is right up there with the giddy laughter of small children or the soft fur of a beloved pet.

1. Understanding your needs: If your husband were to ask you to share your most vulnerable question about your insecurities, what

would you say? What gentle questions do you want to ask him about his insecurities or anxieties? Sharing about our own insecurities can begin a healthy, nonthreatening conversation.

2. Identifying your worth: What's the most powerful question anyone ever asked you? What's the most interesting response you ever got from a question you asked? Please write those two questions in a journal and start a collection of gentle questions. If you're feeling especially generous, send them to me at CathyKrafve.com.

3. Envisioning your future: Many recurring arguments pop up in marriage. Instead of debating, list what you could gently ask your husband next time. If you could have your dream-come-true conversation, what three topics would you include? Ask around among your trusted friends to find some good questions you might ask your hubby in order to bring up one of those three topics soon.

My prayer for you, with my love

Dear God, please bless this beautiful sister's heart with Your wisdom. When she feels she has been treated unjustly by her husband, as all women do sometimes, teach her the best ways to be heard. She may feel isolated and polarized from her hubby sometimes, too. You are the One who waits in joyful anticipation for her to turn to You. You allow her to enter into relationships, knowing they sometimes hurt. We ask for You to bless her with peace and wisdom in her marriage. Teach her to ask questions to spark understanding and unity, not discord.

We praise You for Your faithfulness, as expressed in Psalm 18:35–36: "You have also given me the shield of Your salvation; Your right hand has held me up, Your gentleness has made me great. You enlarged my path under me, So my feet did not slip."

To pray for yourself

Good Father, You are the One who tells me to ask. You promise that my persistent asking opens doors. I receive wisdom because I sought

You out. Show me how I need to approach truth. Teach me to be gentle, humble, and joyful in my understanding. Let me accommodate and respect my husband, rather than polarizing from him. Remind me of my absolute, invaluable worth to You. Teach us to unite around Your purpose for us. Jesus, You describe Yourself as the truth. What better place to turn for answers to my questions? When my husband does not understand my questions, give me the words I need to patiently explain my desire to know him deeply. Give him insight to cherish me. Help us delight in You together. I trust You. Bless me now because that's Your heart's desire. In Jesus' name I pray. Amen.

"To raise new questions, new possibilities, to regard old problems from a new angle, requires creative imagination and marks real advance in science." —Albert Einstein

CHAPTER SIXTEEN

Horses at the Barn

How does hard work unify us?
*By giving us confidence
and a greater sense of purpose.*

Our youngest daughter wanted a horse. We said no. In Texas lots of folks have horses. Horses are a lifestyle with a capital L. Therefore, we knew horses are not like normal pets. For instance, a horse that goes unridden even for a short time goes to seed.

Going to seed is what Texans say when a field gets ignored. Before long, the field's owner is hiring folks to bring in special equipment. A brush hog (I can't make this stuff up) plows through all the stumps from the scrubby underbrush that pops up after a field goes to seed. While horses don't grow wild weeds like a field, horses do grow wild, developing real bad manners quickly. Maybe their instincts kick in because horses think they're free to run wild, like their ancestral mustangs.

In Texas, you can get a good horse pretty cheap, probably because somebody's teenage daughter lost interest when she got a boyfriend in high school. However, trailers, barns, saddles, and riding lessons add up in a hurry. Not to mention weekends spent traveling to rodeos for jumping or barrel racing. Many Texas parents devote so much to their children's dreams, they adopt a lifestyle requiring them to survive with manure in their nostrils every day.

When our daughters realized horses were not part of our life plan, they found another way to develop relationships with four-legged heartthrobs. Soon, both girls worked at a nearby barn. Personally, I have an aversion to any animals bigger than I am but sporting smaller brains. Fortunately, the girls turned into talented wranglers, followed closely by their younger brother. All my kids rib me for my equine fear.

The barn created a separate kingdom for my three children, their own personal Garden of Eden where hard work nurtured its own reward. A haven of four-legged creatures, all just waiting to be named and tamed. Our family owes their cowboy boss, one of the most astute Christian men we know, a debt of gratitude for the lessons he taught our kids while they were all scooping poop together. Cherished mentors, he and his wife bless countless young people year after year with profound daily wisdom.

"What can you tell about a man by the way he treats his animals?" he asked our oldest daughter one day as they drove between fields. She was a teenager at the time, and the question stumped her. I have no idea what she finally answered. Instead, she came home lit up about the genius of a thought-provoking question asked in the cab of a beat-up pickup truck, driving along with the windows rolled down. Wisdom on the way. I am watching her and her hubby with joy and amazement as they apply wisdom on the way to parenting our adorable grandchildren.

Hard Work and the Gift of Joyful Unity

Hard work is a spiritual discipline. When it's applied with wisdom, hard work develops leadership early in the life of a child. True leadership is about service. Good leadership has in mind the best interests of those under authority. The natural byproduct of servant leadership is fellowship.

The same cowboy leader taught our kids to rest by changing jobs at the barn. Never one to endorse boredom, when work seemed like drudgery, he championed a change of pace. Time to change tasks, not wimp out. Good leadership is a joy to behold. Every day our kids stomped through fields in muddy boots and carried fifty-pound bags of grain as if it was pure pleasure for them. David and I are convinced every kid who ever worked for this fine cowboy leader went to their next bosses like prized work horses. The good Lord knows this gentleman wrote enough job references over the years to get some kind of special seating in heaven!

I fear our culture is sending the wrong message to couples, emphasizing fun and leisure over hard work. Both are important. We should not overlook the value of working hard together. Hard work becomes a romantic adventure when you understand the unifying power of shared purpose. David and I went years working in separate jobs, him in the energy business, me at home with kiddos. Our shared purpose of creating a safe home kept us united as we worked in our separate responsibilities during the day.

At night we compared notes. Each morning I thanked David as he left for another day of work. Our weekends always included tasks around the house we could not afford to hire out. So many tasks. Running a household and raising children together requires collaboration.

In recent years, our work allows us to work side by side for the first time in our married life. What a fun adventure for us to finally compile all the small business, organizational, and communication skills we accumulated over a lifetime! But long before we got to form companies together, we discovered the romance and delight in working together to accomplish tasks.

For David and me, two examples of our most romantic memories involve hard work adventures. When we were young and oh-so-strapped financially, we took on the task of building our own cedar privacy fence. In the driving rain, drenched to the skin, we worked together, dedicated to saving money and to the security of our children's backyard.

Another romantic moment involved paddling our decrepit motorboat. Yes, paddling and laughing hysterically together as we sweated under the hot Texas sky. Oh, the absurdity of all our neighbors seeing us from their big windows facing the lake as we paddled along in our latest motorboat calamity! We gave the boat away but kept the stories.

Three things stand out about the spiritual aspect of hard work, 1) hard work unifies couples, families, and communities, 2) hard work makes us grateful, 3) hard work prepares us for whatever the future brings. If you don't mind a little sweat equity, hard work can infuse a marriage with unity, gratefulness, and confidence.

Deep Unity

First, hard work unifies us by teaching us to depend on each other. Difficult tasks quickly teach us the value of help. We learn to count on the strengths of each other to meet needs. Healthy interdependence, not dependence or codependence or independence, fosters a deep unity. When hard work gets hectic, we learn to trust in each other to come through in a pinch.

Nothing creates oneness and emotional connection like sharing a purpose. The harder the challenge, the bigger the goal, the more we see God in the process. Recognizing God in the daily activity of working toward a goal reminds us we are His and under His authority. Being sensitive to His authority ensures our lasting success. Plus, it reinforces our objective of habitually serving each other.

Grateful Hearts

Second, hard work instills gratitude. We tend to take for granted whatever comes to us on a silver platter. In contrast, we treasure accomplishments we work hard to reach. Plus, we appreciate those who worked together to reach our goal.

In a perfect example, the day my dad returned from boot camp made a big impression on me as a small child. Dad, still dressed in his fatigues, flashed a spray of greenbacks, chortling with my happy mom. Since Mom stayed home and managed three small children 24/7 while Dad was gone for National Guard training, she supported his efforts. Together, they rejoiced. Their cash felt like a windfall of community property, a sign of their service to each other. My, what a treat to hold cash in hand when a young family's budget strained! I suspect he cashed his paycheck in ones to make her laugh.

Gratitude cures bitterness like penicillin cures disease. Nothing makes us more grateful than a team we can count on. No one can doubt the team-building genius of Vince Lombardi who said, "The price of success is hard work, dedication to the job at hand, and the determination that whether we win or lose, we have applied the best of ourselves to the task at hand."[36] Applying our best includes looking for ways to express gratitude for our marriage by serving together wholeheartedly. Bitterness melts away as we gratefully respect each other's hard work.

Confidently Pressing on Together

Third, hard work provides hope for the future. We learn to trust God in the present with difficult challenges. We gain confidence by knowing what is true and doing what is hard. Working hard together as a couple unifies a family, teaching us to press on with confidence when life gets tough, as it inevitably will.

Whenever I think of wisdom and confidence, I immediately think of the Proverbs. I keep a paperback Bible next to my exercise bike, specifically for studying Proverbs. I color-code by topics. Color-coding seems kinda nerdy I know, but it gives me a chance to play with neon highlighters. Plus, it's fun to read each one of the thirty-one proverbs daily. I repeat them each month. I figure if I park my brain in Proverbs long enough, maybe I'll be wise someday.

In Proverbs, we discover again how inseparably linked financial gain and hard work are to correction and wisdom. I pulled the following gem especially for you; it seemed providential since it mentioned barns.

"Honor the LORD with your possessions, And with the firstfruits of all your increase; So your barns will be filled with plenty, And your vats will overflow with new wine. My son, do not despise the chastening of the LORD, Nor detest His correction; For whom the LORD loves He corrects, Just as a father the son *in whom* he delights. Happy *is* the man *who* finds wisdom, And the man *who* gains understanding; For

---

36 Vince Lombardi, http://www.brainyquote.com/quotes/keywords/hard_work.html, accessed 02-08-17.

her proceeds *are* better than the profits of silver, And her gain than fine gold" (Proverbs 3:9–14).

I turned to Proverbs 3 since I happened to be writing this chapter on the third day of the month, but Proverbs grants gems every day.

I want you to know that God stays continually aware of your hard work. He loves you because you are His own child. He instructs us and disciplines us as His beloved children. Just like our kids' cowboy boss, God often gently counsels us, and sometimes we don't even know it happened. Proverbs is loaded with wisdom about work and everyday life for anytime we feel taken for granted.

Clear the Deck

Work is so hard, sometimes the greatest challenge is to prioritize. How do I say no to some things and prioritize what's necessary? Aha! That has to be the raging question for this generation of young moms. *No* could be our best word. Maybe that's why God programed us to learn it first as toddlers.

The hardest work we do in marriages, or any relationship, is unloading all the emotional baggage that keeps us from joining in together enthusiastically. Having a content heart and a happy life starts by asking ourselves what God designed us for. Equipped with His purpose for our lives, we say no to everything else. Putting a family purpose statement into words helps clear the deck of all superfluous commitments. It's so much better to wake up believing our days will be spent on the things that matter most to us and to God.

When we talk about working hard, remember God designed work to bless, so we want to focus on relevant work and let everything irrelevant go. We don't want to be guilty of doing the jobs God designed for someone else. We want to focus on the work God intends to create unity for us as a couple. By responding to His Spirit as we choose our day's activities, we will naturally draw others to Him as we go along.

To me, the blessings of hard work are summed up in the word unity. As a wife, I know how shame and frustration can short-circuit a marriage for years. Sometimes the hardest challenges include understanding what was not said. We could forgive if only we understood.

Marriage is multifaceted, challenging emotional work because we are multifaceted, complex human beings with physical, emotional, and spiritual needs. Often, we can't even identify our needs for ourselves much less for others.

The Hard Work of Physical, Emotional, and Spiritual Insight

Standing next to your husband on a special project, like building a fence in the pouring rain, offers you insight you can't get any other way. Hard work provides an opportunity to cherish the one you love in all his complexities. It's another way to share your most intimate self as you overcome challenges together. Hard work, with its process of sharing and serving, enhances fellowship in a deeply spiritual way.

Personally, I'll take any little hint about how to understand my husband better. Marriage communication is hard work. When we work on a project together, especially outside, we encounter a whole new level of communication, including body language, facial expressions, and grunts we might not experience anywhere else. Yes, grunts. When we work outside, I only have energy left for grunts at the end of the day.

Working together on a big outdoor project means less talk and more body language. For women who are gifted with the ability to read people, this may seem obvious. But for me, learning to read my husband's unspoken signals was a challenge.

I learned a thing or two about body language from the wranglers at my house. Our middle daughter soon discovered her special knack for reading the horses' body language. From her, we learned horses communicate with a shake of the mane, a shoulder nudge, a tail flip, a stamped hoof, or a snort. Like humans, horses often jockey for position. A quick study of the herd reveals the various roles of each horse.

It's clear horses feel good about working hard to provide rides, although they will complain when riders are inept. In fact, a horse will refuse to serve a rider who sends mixed messages. Horses have great instincts. It never pays to sneak up on one.

When the day is done, the whole herd rushes to return to the safety of the barn. Once their saddles are removed, they joyfully receive their brushing. They bury their velvety noses in tin buckets hung all around the walls of the barn and munch on their hard-earned reward of oats. After dinner, they frisk and play in the open fields as the sun sets and the stars come out.

Just like a herd of horses delights in togetherness after a hard day, humans discover hard work creates an atmosphere of gratitude and satisfaction. In our families, hard work unifies us with confidence and a sense of purpose and pleasure.

Hard work is a blessing created for us before the fall when the Garden of Eden was the sweetest spot on earth. God designed the garden as a haven. Then, God did Adam a huge favor and announced an important truth. "And the LORD God said, '*It is* not good that man should be alone; I will make him a helper comparable to him'" (Genesis 2:18).

Against the beautiful backdrop of a garden tended by Adam with Eve's help, the Almighty Creator strolled with them in peaceful unity, admiring the fruit of their labor together. I pray your home is a haven as you work side by side.

In Case You Were Wondering...

How do I balance being confident about what I am good at, while being vulnerable and humble about everything else? Through interdependence. Not dependence. Not codependence. Not independence. Just good old give-and-take. Enjoying what we have to give others frees us. We can enjoy with gratitude the marvelous strengths others bring to the table.

By the way, don't discount weaknesses in the mix. Weaknesses are the glue holding us together and making us grateful. Gratefulness is the picture of unity in action.

Hard work stretches us to love both our strengths and our weaknesses. God loves us just the same way, in our strengths and our weaknesses. He shows Himself to be strong in our weaknesses. One of my favorite examples of how God strengthens those He loves and understands human fear is in Isaiah, "Fear not, for I *am* with you; Be not dismayed, for I *am* your God. I will strengthen you, Yes, I will help you, I will uphold you with My righteous right hand" (Isaiah 41:10).

As families branch out to dream big, we all face hard work. Oh, to be the wife and mother who shares God's heart for those she loves. *I stand with you. How can I help? Do not be afraid. I have confidence in you. Your hard work will pay off. I am proud of you.* These are the messages we wish to share with our husband, our kids, and our grandchildren.

Pause, Ponder, Pray, and then Proceed

We know work is hard, but we tend to forget that work is intended as a blessing. All tasks can conform to a creative, loving purpose by simplifying. Let's take our questions about hard work to God, the One who created for six days and then rested.

1. Understanding your needs: What hard work would you be willing to take on in order to gain a more unified, intimate understanding of yourself and your husband? Consider removing some items from your schedule to make time for a project you could do together as a couple. Like the horses in the barn, what positive body language have you noticed being communicated subconsciously in your home?

2. Identifying your worth: In your life currently, which hard activities make you want to romp and play like a frisky horse after work? How can you build more of those activities into your family life? An overcrowded schedule is the enemy of priorities. No need to add false guilt to your day. Instead, watch for chances to clear some time for your family's priorities.

3. Envisioning your future: At the end of the day, when all the hard work is done, where do you retreat to relax? Create a space to relax and refresh yourself, maybe a stuffed chair or a warm bathtub full of bubbles. When you think about your best relationships, how do those friends keep you on track? What distractions can you eliminate? Eliminating distractions can be tricky, but oh-so rewarding.

My prayer for you, with my love

Dear God, the One who gave us work as a blessing, please take notice of my sister. Hard working women often face exhaustion, Lord. Folks can label us in unkind ways. As we work hard, we find ourselves disappointed when our efforts go unnoticed. Empower this dear sister to honor You by collaborating well with those she loves. Help her to see the value of both her strengths and her weaknesses.

Let her recognize the value she adds to the life of everyone around her. Show her what's best for her family.

With the words of Psalm 19:14, we honor You: "Let the words of my mouth and the meditation of my heart Be acceptable in Your sight, O LORD, my strength and my Redeemer."

To pray for yourself

Good Father, the One who worked and rested, You know when the sun rises and when it sets. Please replace any exhaustion I feel with pure joy. Let me rest peacefully, trusting You. You set the stars in motion. You measure the oceans in Your hand. You are powerful enough to take care of me. Let my hard work be a blessing to my husband. Give us work we can do together with joyful unity of purpose. Let my words of praise for my husband go straight to his heart. May my confidence be grounded in Your leadership and love for me. Teach me to know what's true and to do what's hard. Let my hard work be honoring to You, O Lord, my strength and my Redeemer. Let my heart continually praise You, O Provider of my soul! Bless me now because that's Your heart's desire. In Jesus' name I pray. Amen.

"Praying hard is two dimensional: praying like it depends on God, and working like it depends on you." —**Mark Batterson**, from *The Circle Maker*

CHAPTER SEVENTEEN

The Compassion Story

How does respecting free will put our hearts at rest?
By freeing us to pray rather than judge.

We sat on the couch together, holding hands and looking into each other's eyes. How would he respond, with rejection, judgement, or condemnation? Was he going to regret marrying me? Would he want a divorce?

Up until that moment, I never said *abortion* out loud. The word had a magic power over me. Even years after the event, I felt like hiding, always ready to dodge the topic. When we fell in love, I didn't have the nerve to tell this wonderful man about my past. I devoted myself to living in the present without looking back. But it wasn't easy.

In the 1980s, every sermon seemed devoted to the wrongs of abortion. Each Sunday, I sat in the pew, ready to run for the bathroom, feeling like I would vomit. I tried hard to forget, but I remembered the smell of the pungent cleanser they used at the clinic and the weird way the light bulbs reflected my anxiety.

After the abortion, I dramatically changed my lifestyle, determined to avoid repeating my mistake. I quit dating. Instead, I began building friendships. However, as David and I moved toward a serious relationship, my unspoken fears haunted me.

I knew I owed him the truth. Yet, somehow, the conversation always evaporated before it started. How could I marry him when I could not tell him about my past? Compassion is one reason I knew I could marry David. Intuitively, I believed David would forgive me for keeping the secret.

About four years after we married, I began to have symptoms related to lingering abortion trauma, called Post Abortion Syndrome. Of course, I needed serious counseling. By then, I held two beautiful toddlers in my lap. But holding them was beginning to hurt my soul because of the baby I never held. Unspoken grief was robbing me of joy with my children.

Eventually, I sought help. After weeks of sitting on her couch, sobbing and struggling to forgive myself, my counselor spoke a truth into my life I will never forget.

"Cathy, I admire your courage."

No one had ever admired my courage before. Steadying my wounded soul, I searched deeply for the courage I needed for a life-changing conversation. Finally, the day came when I would tell David.

I held my breath for a moment, then exhaled and told him about my abortion. Instead of rejecting me, David tenderly wrapped his arms around me. Then he said the most loving words I believe I've ever heard.

"I am so sorry you had to go through that."

Right then and there, my heart began to heal in its most sacred, yet wounded place. If this good man, the father of our young children, could forgive me and still cherish me, perhaps God truly loved me unconditionally as well. Was there ever better evidence of God's own mercy and grace toward me?

I call this the "Compassion Story."[37] Compassion, especially self-compassion, frees us to live with joy in the present.

Free Will and Judgement

Humans don't always use good judgement in the choices we make. When friends flirt with heartache, we see danger ahead. Should we

---

37 Debra L. Butterfield, *Abba's Answers*, "The Compassion Story," (St. Joseph, MO: CrossRiver Media, 2020), 17.

warn them of the threat? Sometimes we choose to warn them, but they ignore our pleadings. We may argue and cry. We've all been there.

The words "to judge" get a bad rap. We've all read verses like "Judge not, that you be not judged" (Matthew 7:1). But why not judge? Unlike condemnation, good judgment is a terrific thing. Perhaps it's because we use the words *judge* and *condemn* almost synonymously.

Certainly, we can evaluate a situation wisely without condemning the other person. All the while, we somehow have to live with others who test the limits of our compassion.

Compassion says, I *know you and love you even though you and I are both sinners.* We need to forgive ourselves in order to get to the place where we can love others with compassion. Nowhere is this process of mutual self-forgiveness more crucial than in our marriage.

In marriage, we must make wise analysis of problems we may face. To judge can be a way of discerning. We want to let go of condemning. Yet, we all have a tendency to choose condemnation, sort of like small children tend to want justice until they find out it applies to them.

When we condemn, we take on the role of judge. Like a life sentence, condemnation declares a permanent state of unworthiness or failure of character. Jesus is the only righteous judge. We should wait for Him to clarify all things.

For example, I can easily offer a word of encouragement to young women in unplanned pregnancies because I have been there. Or for those like me, who chose abortion, I know how to comfort and console since I received forgiveness, comfort, and consolation myself.

We all know from personal experience how painful consequences can be. Even when we disagree with others' decisions, we offer understanding. This is an especially valuable gift to give a husband. Compassion and patience strengthen and encourage a husband as he wrestles with tough decisions required for the well-being of his family.

The High Value of Free Will

One thing is clear, God relishes our free will. In fact, God loves free will so much, He gave it His own valuable endorsement. How do we know God puts His stamp of approval on our free will? Because He could have made us as puppets or robots, obeying Him without question. Since humans are not robots, our God-given free will means we will inevitably mess up.

I love what Romans 5:8 says, "But God demonstrates His own love toward us, in that while we were still sinners, Christ died for us." Knowing we would choose sin, God provided for our free will in advance in the life, death, and resurrection of His own beloved Son. That's some endorsement of the value of free will!

Perhaps even more revealing, we see Jesus demonstrate the struggle between following our own free will and embracing God's plan for us. Before He went to the cross, Jesus prayed, "Father, if it is Your will, take this cup away from Me; nevertheless not My will, but Yours, be done" (Luke 22:42).

God's will in my life always includes the best interest of others, as Jesus' own choice demonstrates. Jesus died on the cross for sin, proof God puts a high value on our free will, even knowing our lives would get messy sometimes.

When I say God endorses our free will, I don't say so lightly. Unlike robots, our free will means humans can make choices to respect God or reject Him. Wow! No wonder we humans throw the word *choice* around with so much passion!

Just think! God wants us to choose Him, so He provided ahead of time for our foolhardy, selfish choices. However, the time comes when we no longer get to choose. Death closes the door on all our decision-making power. Don't let that moment sneak up on you. Choose God now.

Choosing Prayer as an Act of Love

We can intercede on behalf of those we love through prayer when we recognize the dangerous consequences of injudicious decisions. We respect their choices, all the while praying fervently. We choose prayer as an act of love, a patient expression of our faithful devotion. We pray

God will protect them as the consequences unfold.

Since God freely offers us liberty to enjoy, we want to avoid taking free will to its destructive end. There's an old word for when people try to take advantage of God's grace, license. Just like James Bond has a license to kill, sometimes people think they have a license to sin. The British government may give spies permission to break the law in fiction, but in real life, sin has consequences.

License for the Christian means intentionally choosing destructive behaviors because we know Jesus offers forgiveness. I am not spouting some cheap brand of license here.

Foolish self-centeredness is destructive and dangerous. A great example might be the person who drinks and drives, selfishly wanting to party while putting everyone else at risk. When we notice those we love making foolish choices, we groan with fear for their welfare. Prayer can be an expensive and sacrificial gift in those moments.

Sometimes, as we pray for others, our own heart comes under conviction. Nothing puts the spotlight on our own bad attitudes and behaviors quicker than praying for others. Oh, how I hate it when I find myself convicted about my own sinful attitude! Prayer often corrects the prayer warrior first.

Consequences: the friend of free Will

Consequences are God's partner in helping us find His healthy, wholehearted path. They are the friend of our free will. God demonstrates He loves us and respects our choices by designing consequences. All young mommies know this because consequences are the friend of every good parent and the bane of a toddler's existence.

An unavoidable self-correcting force of nature, consequences release us from feeling we need to over-protect other adults. We soon discover good consequences *confirm* good behavior and bad consequences *correct* selfish behavior. The power in consequences means we can enjoy our spouse, even when they make decisions we don't like.

Entering into Others' Pain with Compassion

Sooner or later, consequences catch up with all of us. Fortunately, prayer allows us to seek help and protection from the loving God Almighty. The principle of respecting free will can powerfully transform families.

When I told David about my abortion, for example, he didn't have to remind me what I did was unbiblical, a sin. I knew by snuffing out the life of my unborn child I dishonored and misrepresented God's unfailing love. David recognized I was still experiencing the painful consequences of a decision I made years earlier. He simply entered into my pain with compassion.

As we follow Jesus, we can enter into others' pain with compassion. The day will come when Jesus will rightly judge us, whether we chose a relationship with Him or not. Until then, He Himself refrains from condemning us, instead letting consequences take their natural corrective and confirming course in our lives (John 8:11).

Nowhere is compassion more trustworthy than in our marriages. Truly, we are wise to offer not only compassion, but empathy as well, since we are fellow sinners. In fact, without compassion, relationships are nearly impossible. Nothing kills authentic conversation faster than condemnation.

Marriage: Still a Controversial Topic

Marriage has been a controversial subject for centuries, but lately with the same-sex discussion, families are struggling to adjust to modern perspectives. There's been so much hoopla in the media about same-sex marriage, you might think mankind just thought up a new way to torture parents. Even though this book is primarily written for heterosexual women, this is my chance to offer a word of encouragement to all.

I know so many parents whose adult children make choices they don't understand. Do you reject the child because they choose a lifestyle you believe is wrong? My own personal opinion is no, you do not. Why? Because God's grace to us is an expression of His long-suffering love. Besides, blasphemy manifests itself in our own lives when we take over Jesus' role as righteous judge.

For those families struggling with the issue of same-sex marriage, I admire your courage. In a book about marriage, I feel God would love to see us talk compassionately about the subject of same-sex marriages. If you will bear with me, I would love to try to give some persuasive ways to talk to a whole generation who are drowning in this topic of trying to redefine marriage.

I'm always a little sad when I hear people define themselves by their sexual appetites. It's so much better to look to the future with understanding about the real underlying reason compelling us. We are given a transitory moment in time on this earth as a prelude to unending eternity. How much better to embrace an unchanging definition of our true identity. Each and every one of us is a human with a spirit.

Sexual appetites are transitory by their nature. For instance, with all couples, sexual appetites ebb and flow. Many circumstances can change the trajectory of our sex life. The birth of a baby, depression, porn addictions, trauma, health crises, even the natural aging process, among many other factors, all seem to conspire against our sex life. Why define oneself by something that is so transitory?

It is easy to write off relationships because we disagree. It is easy to say, "You're wrong." Condemning is the coward's way out. God calls us to mend the brokenhearted, to comfort those in pain.

Craving the Eternal

Telling people homosexuality is sin is *not* helping apparently, since it seems more and more kids are persuaded to define themselves by their sexual appetites. Remember, sin is simply testifying something false about God with our lifestyle. When young people—or older ones—define their identity by something so transitory as sexual appetites, they misrepresent God's greater eternal purpose in our lives.

God seeks us. He offers eternal companionship in His unfailing, unchanging love. When we come together male and female, we represent the complementary, cohesive nature of God Himself. Sexual cravings are merely a temporal, physical picture of an eternal spiritual reality. Physical cravings fall away, even as does our appetite for food as we get nearer to death. But the craving for the eternal grows.

The topic of same sex marriage deserves its own book by authorities far more experienced and brave than me. All I want to add to the discussion is this: Don't rush to judge and condemn. Pause, pray, and ponder. Make room in your heart to try to understand. There are hurts and proclivities so deep only God can measure the pain rightly. We may never understand what drives the ones we love to seek affection in ways we find difficult.

I feel it's rare for people who define themselves as homosexual to be so vulnerable with folks who, like me, believe homosexuality is not an identity but an appetite. If your adult children are willing to talk to you gently, please savor the opportunity, even if their perspectives leave you gasping for air. While you are together cherish the ways you can spend time together.

If someone in your family threatens to abandon your relationship because you do not agree with their perspective, you may need a mutual break. Threatening to abandon a relationship, especially over lifestyle or religious differences of opinion, is manipulative.

Yet, God does not manipulate us. He paid the price for our free will. Civilized people with even the most divergent perspectives can spend time together in a cafe or volunteer activity. If possible, schedule a time to revisit hot topics when tempers are cooler. Consider sowing seeds of mutual respect around God's love of our free will. Above all, please remember our identities are simple: All people are humans with a spirit. Begin there.

Since marriage is God's domain, we don't have to be shocked or dismayed when other people make choices based on their own free will. We can confidently embrace Jesus' definition of marriage. All the while, we can love people where they are, knowing there's always more to everyone's story.

Since God's way of leading includes compassion, we trust compassion as a good strategy for us as well. I love the way one friend eloquently summed up condemnation when I asked for her input for this book. "The result of our trying to do God's job rather than act as Christ's follower, is that we have created an entire community of hurting people, seeking the sense of belonging and emotional safety we all seek as humans. Rather than being pulled into the church and loved to Christ, they are being isolated, hurt, shamed, excluded, *preached at* instead of *ministered to* and as a result, are driven (by self-preservation) away. The church should be the very place where we nurture the most, using kindness as a way of leading others to Christ." Gently, we must offer compassionate solutions to the pain we see in lives all around us.

Consequences Correct and Confirm

Demanding that people agree with us is not likely to persuade. Encouraging others to build their life on biblical principles will be more persuasive as we live out the sacrificial, self-respecting worthiness God designed us to enjoy. Often the controlling, selfish compulsions I feel are rooted in woundedness from my own past. I'm truly grateful my husband has the compassionate patience to sort out my motivations with me.

Those who choose the difficult path of compassion deeply respect God's choice to give us a free will. People have the right to make the decisions they choose, even the ones with which we disagree. Even when choices prove self-destructive. Until the moment when Jesus rightly judges all of us once and for all, let us watch, pray, and love unfailingly.

Dave's choice to grant me compassion when I told him about my abortion set a tried-and-true trajectory for our marriage. In spite of many sticking points, including countless communication handicaps, I knew the relationship was worth fighting for. Years later, as we renegotiated our marriage, all I could think of was this: "Where could I ever find another man to love me with that kind of compassion?" Compassion can make a marriage worth saving. What a powerful force for good in the world!

I am sensitive to women who have experienced abuse in their marriage, so I feel I must again reiterate, compassion alone cannot heal some marriages. In fact, a wife's most compassionate choice may be to get out of the way while her husband experiences the serious consequences of his choices, including divorce. Remember, God set consequences in motion with your husband's best interest in mind, as well as yours. Consequences are evidence of God's long-suffering, grace-powered mercy extended to all of us.

Contentment and a Cup of Coffee

Can you guess why I really love consequences so much? Because I get to let go of my over-responsible burden of taking care of, well, everyone. Fortunately, respecting free will means we are not required to babysit adults. In fact, adults will be better off if we don't babysit them.

I don't have to be the expert on how others live. Thank goodness, I get to focus on contentment instead. Yep, we are all needy in our own unique ways, so it's okay to expect adults to grow up. We are not required to step in and fix their lives for them. Phew! That's a relief.

Patience with others and contentment within our current circumstances can be serious challenges. Contentment, at my house at least, looks like a Saturday morning with a cup of coffee and nowhere to go.

Modern women can take a minute and catch our breath. Certainly, it's okay to quit striving and chill. Having compassion on ourselves and our families may mean taking a few minutes of down time to reboot our emotional health. Emotional well-being may require respecting the decisions made by those we love, even the bad decisions.

With the help of a truthful friend, I began to observe when I felt discontent. I started intentionally focusing on being content instead. As I perused the Scriptures, I noticed a pattern. Contentment begins and ends with gratitude. Gratitude is a free will choice, a very powerful one.

In place of competing, correcting, condemning, or controlling in our marriages, we can choose gratitude and contentment. Choose wisely! Compassion allows families to gratefully acknowledge God as the one source of forgiveness and freedom.

In the next chapter, we'll dig into consequences further for those times when marriage feels like a one-horse carriage. Women commonly feel like they are pulling the whole load alone until all their energy seems to evaporate. Poof! Often, they hung in there because of their kids.

Stay tuned because there's hope for your kids, even in the worst of circumstances. No matter your situation, you can still model healthy relationships for your children. Creating great marriage conversations means learning to cherish all our relationships. What a lovely inheritance to pass along to those you love!

In Case You Were Wondering...

What about when my husband unjustly accuses me of bad attitudes, even if my attitude is fine? Injustice hurts a lot and makes us mad. Don't I know it! My feelings are hypersensitive, especially anywhere my hubby is concerned. But we can expect to be misjudged sometimes because humans do misjudge. A lot, actually.

If we understand what a high price Jesus paid for our free will, we set ourselves free from the tendency to condemn. If your husband makes a habit of misjudging you, you may need to seek a counselor's advice. Some forms of abuse, like gaslighting for instance, are signaled by false accusations. If it's a rare occasion when you misjudge each other, then there are some steps you can try before rushing to make your next appointment on the counselor's couch.

Begin by asking a bunch of gentle diagnostic questions to reboot conversation again. Whatever you do, don't assume and argue. Instead, ask questions and pray a lot. Please know this—God is in favor of your marriage. He respects your free will and your husband's.

If a husband truly misjudges, (I should write *when*), appeal to a higher court. What an effective prayer! God, the Righteous Judge, loves to answer prayers about injustice!

Pause, Ponder, Pray, and then Proceed

As women, we ought to treat our own hearts with compassion first.

When those we love break our hearts, as they sometimes do, we will then be able to pass along the same comfort God gives us.

1. Understanding your needs: How has free will been a blessing and a curse in your life? List the ways the enemy of your soul tries to lie to you. Where do you need to begin embracing the compassion God offers you? Today let your free will be a blessing to someone else by choosing to speak a kind word where it's unexpected.

2. Identifying your worth: When your heart yearns to extend compassion, especially to your husband, what keeps you from doing so? Who in your life embodies compassion? This week, pick up a small habit from a compassionate friend and extend it to your hubby.

3. Envisioning your future: If God were to instantly heal the hurting relationships in your life, how would their healing affect your future? Please extend compassion to someone this week simply because God loves you. If you made it a habit to offer your husband daily doses of compassion starting today, how could your marriage look in five months? In five years? Please prepare a little dose of compassion with your dinner tonight, perhaps with a gentle question as you sit down to eat.

My prayer for you, with my love

Dear God, the One who paid the ultimate price for free will, please help this dear sister value hers. Where her heart is wounded, heal her with Your tender compassion. Sometimes as women we grieve and feel inconsolable. Our hurts can be debilitating. Help her love herself unconditionally and compassionately, free of shame and guilt. Help her extend the same kind of mercy to all those she loves, especially her husband.

Together we kneel before You, O, Compassionate Lord, and claim, "A posterity shall serve Him. It will be recounted of the Lord to the *next* generation, They will come and declare His righteousness to a people who will be born, That He has done *this*" (Psalm 22:30–31).

To pray for yourself:

Good Father, You do not mess around, but instead paid the full price for my free will, even my most serious and willful mistakes. In my grief, You comfort me. My heart trembles in gratitude when I consider the danger my free will presents. This is difficult for me because I am constantly tempted to give myself more credit than I deserve. At the same time, I blame myself for everything in the universe. Have mercy on this poor confused soul, Lord! When I feel inconsolable, You tenderly console me again and again.

Help me bite my tongue and compassionately love my husband today. Teach me to respect You by respecting others. You are so good to me. Help my heart trust Your loving embrace. Bless me now because that's Your heart's desire. In Jesus' name I pray. Amen.

"Love and compassion are necessities, not luxuries. Without them humanity cannot survive." —**Dalai Lama**

CHAPTER EIGHTEEN

Don't Be an Island

If my marriage suffered, how can I regroup so my kids don't suffer?

We model for our children how to turn unavoidable suffering into joy-filled peace.

my sister and I cringed at each lightning strike as we watched the storm roar outside our window. From our twin beds like matching rowboats, we felt awash in an ocean of fear. I remember fear upon fear piling up like the crests of rising water outside as the evening darkened in a crashing storm. Where could our parents be?

We waved goodbye to our parents earlier in the morning, with no foreshadowing of the danger ahead. We welcomed a favorite babysitter, a rare treat. My parents left for a fun afternoon with their friends at a nearby beach house. Sunshine sparkled all around us.

Near Bolivar Peninsula, the storm materialized out of nowhere. Unable to see more than a few feet on any side, the rain drummed over the boat in a sheet-like drenching. With the boat's owner, my mom struggled to hold tightly to the small sailboat always on the verge of collapse.

They experienced real terror; danger threatened to wash them both away from their young families. Then, miraculously, quiet broke through the storm, and a motorboat appeared with my dad, searching frantically for them. In spite of the double risk of leaving his kids as orphans in the same awful storm, he refused to call off the search. I suspect he was a hero, not only to our family, but also to the young wife and children of their friend.

How relieved we were when they finally reappeared at home, exhausted and dripping! Years later, Mom told me how closely we came to losing her that day. By then, I had a young family of my own. I easily imagined the tragedy of a young husband and no mommy, with their three little ones, my siblings and me.

We left Galveston after Dad finished his medical training. Our family settled in Tyler, a lovely small town surrounded by pine trees and securely away from hurricanes, a benefit I endorsed even as a small child.

A Front Row Seat for Suffering

Marriage can feel like a lonely island in a raging storm of insecurity. Divorce is one serious way to suffer, but not the only one. Kids have a front row seat for it all.

Twenty-five or so years into their marriage, while I was a college student, Mom called to tell me she and Dad were struggling to hold their marriage together. I guess I responded intuitively.

"Let's go to Galveston, Mom," I said, "We can have a girls' weekend and just hang out."

Mom and I checked into a crumbling hotel near the sea wall; our room smelled of mold. Once a modern hotel where I learned to swim, disrepair best described it when Mom and I checked in for our nostalgic retreat. On that trip I realized I don't like sharing hotel rooms with roaches.

When the weekend came to a close, she went home and I went back to college. I don't know exactly what happened after Mom got home to Tyler. I guess Mom and Dad talked heart-to-heart. They must have talked about what they wanted their marriage to look like. Perhaps some negotiating happened. Things settled down. Mom continued to hang in there. Within a few years Dad joined AA. Things got a lot better.

At the worst crisis point, my brother was still in high school. Mom always gratefully acknowledged the loving way he encouraged her through that time. I try to imagine what it was like for my brother to watch our parents struggle.

When David and I struggled, our kids were a source of inspiration for us. Every parent desires for their child to create an amazing, happy, lasting marriage. No one wants to give up on a marriage.

In those moments while Dave and I were struggling, it never entered my mind I was modeling a skill set my children might need someday. Instead, as parents, we hope to give our kids skills to prevent a marriage from unraveling. Somehow, we imagine a fairy tale ending for them, even knowing all humans face many of the same struggles.

Don't Isolate, Seek Help

While the children often have a front row seat to suspect problems in a marriage, friends may be caught by surprise. Sometimes people I know get divorced seemingly without any warning. This always bugs me. We always ought to give true friends a chance to pray for us, talk some sense into us, step up on our behalf, or offer comfort in a marriage crisis. Anything.

Sometimes even the wife doesn't see it coming. No matter. Whatever you do, don't isolate. Compassionate help is out there, if we seek it. The places we most expect compassion may fail us. The places we least expect compassion may surprise us. Keep seeking.

We should not cut our close friends out of the opportunity to help us. Especially when children are affected, we owe it to ourselves and them to reach out for help where it may be found. We all wish we could protect our children from crisis, but that is illogical. Not every marriage can be saved or needs to be. Unexpected challenges make up life. It's better to prepare our children to weather life's storms.

By the way, many of my closest friends were affected by divorce, seemingly swamping marriages like a tidal wave in the late '70s and early '80s. I've been told by strong believers that your parents' divorce scars you for the rest of your life. I don't doubt it, but I know these same friends have some of the sweetest fellowship-based marriages I know. Perhaps the accidental and intentional lessons their parents taught them contribute today to the tender and loving way they cherish their own marriages. I offer the thoughts in this chapter as hope and encouragement.

Our family weathered some serious storms on Galveston Island when I was a child. I still prefer higher ground when it rains—higher ground on the mainland. Still, storms on islands, like roaches in hotel rooms, can't always be avoided.

When storms hit your marriage, as they inevitably will, you will be glad if you have cultivated fellowship in deeply rooted relationships with your kids and a few close friends. I'm not a counselor, but I'm told if your husband tries to cut you off from friends and family, that's a big red flag. Don't choose to make your life a deserted island. Please seek professional help or advice from a clergy if your marriage needs attention, especially if you feel isolated.

Rich and Poignant Gratitude

Instead of isolation, choose to live vulnerably, openly, and courageously with those you love. Storms tend to change our perspective. Surviving a storm makes us grateful. Choosing joyful gratitude, especially through crisis, sets the stage for your children's future success.

I don't remember much else about our weekend in Galveston, except that Mom and I were both sad, but the fellowship was rich and poignant. There was comfort in being together. I didn't know then that she was already teaching me what I would someday need in my own life. I bet she didn't know it either. She was just being real and courageous. She needed comfort and loving companionship. I was honored to offer both.

Thinking back, I wonder now if my dad's early heroic sailboat rescue moment framed the trajectory of their marriage. Did Mom wonder later when their marriage hit a snag, *Who else could love me like that?*

God Is Your Defender

God offers us life-saving help. This is especially true when our children suffer. Often, when a man fails at being an attentive husband, he also fails at being a dad. I am proud of you for your courage, especially if you are recognizing your kids' needs in the midst of your own pain, anger, and heartbreak.

Their dad's lack of attention, even abandonment, adds another injustice to you as well. God is your Defender, and the kids' dad would be wise to keep that in mind. But often men don't. They have their own wounds. Thankfully, consequences have a way of correcting all of us. May I tenderly encourage you to put aside anger before it turns to bitterness and depression. Forgiving your husband, or ex-husband, for neglecting the children takes a special dispensation of holy-glory-hallelujah mercy. Yet, forgiveness and grace are your best hope of freeing your children.

If you can't do it for yourself, do it for them. Don't pretend. Instead, keep practicing forgiveness until you believe it yourself because it's true. I like what Debra L. Butterfield said when she came on Fireside Talk Radio.

"So often I hear about forgiveness as being a process, but forgiveness is a choice of your free will. It's a decision you make," Deb explains. "Now, it takes time for your emotions to catch up with that decision." We may find ourselves coming back to powerful emotions over and over again, according to Deb. Yet, she is clear about forgiveness.

"The first time I chose to forgive him, he was forgiven. So, it's not like it's a process where the forgiveness grows," Deb emphasizes, "It's a free will choice." [38]

Honestly, even though we know Jesus died on the cross to extend forgiveness, ouch, it can be so hard to forgive. Especially when their dad continues to make the same mistakes.

In the meantime, you are astute if you recognize your kids' anger, too. Most people don't identify frustration or annoyance or passive aggressive behaviors as low-grade anger and pain. Perhaps you are dealing with rage, fury, and self-destructive tendencies. Your own and your kids'.

Search for help at church or a local nonprofit for the counsel you and your children need. The process may feel overwhelming. Please persist.

---

38 Debra L. Butterfield, Fireside Talk Radio, "Carried By Grace: When Sexual Abuse Happens in Your Home with Deb Butterfield, Her Wisdom," July 13, 2020

Because families create taboos about negative feelings, anger can disguise itself in interesting ways. "I'm just frustrated," folks say when they may feel rage or fury. You are on a healthy path by recognizing your children are experiencing pain and anger. With deep gratitude, we've interviewed a bunch of experts on Fireside Talk Radio; check there for any podcasts related to mental, physical, emotional, and spiritual well-being.

If you are struggling in your marriage or have experienced divorce, your children can still succeed in their marriages as they witness your perseverance, humility, and courage. They will witness the rich and poignant nature of your grateful heart refined in suffering. Your children are by no means doomed to repeat any mistakes they watched their parents make.

By demonstrating tender openness and forgiveness, you are setting them up for success and healing. One thing I learned in Galveston—when all looks lost, victory is sweeter still.

In Case You Were Wondering...

When is it okay to say no? More than any other place in our lives, saying no to our husbands for the sake of our children is the single hardest thing we're called to do.

Sometimes, saying no to your husband changes the dynamics enough to create a shift. Every family needs a shift sometimes or even a chain reaction of small positive shifts. But not all shifts are minor ones.

A friend once told me we are all in crisis, but some of us don't know it yet. Even when our marriages unravel, our hearts don't have to come unglued.

You will feel more comfortable saying no if you nail down your priorities. Your first loyalty is to God, then your hubby, then your kids. But what if your husband does not consider their best interests as he treats you disrespectfully? It may be up to you to put your foot down. That can create quite a storm.

If your husband fails to meet his mandate to protect the children and train them, particularly in respecting his wife, the responsibility shifts to your shoulders. God wants everyone in your family to be safe and sound. You are teaching your kids habits to serve them for a lifetime. Mutual respect is crucial to their future success.

Do the things God has for you. Say no to the rest. Fortunately, as we weather life's sorrows together, we teach our children valuable lessons. Our family still praises my mom for the myriad of ways she demonstrated courage and perseverance. Your beautiful strength, courage, and integrity will get passed down to future generations.

Pause, Ponder, Pray, and then Proceed

I am convinced through strategic prayer we see miracles. Through prayer we tear down strongholds and heal wounds, freeing our families for generations to come.

1. Understanding your needs: If a magic wand could create one exceedingly good thing for your children, what would it be? In your most faith-filled moments, what do you ask God to do for you and your children? What is so gigantic you are afraid to ask God for it? Ask anyway.

2. Identifying your worth: Which of your friends prays and gets results? Make a list and ask that friend to pray for you. What have you been putting off because you felt like you couldn't afford it? Ask God to provide a little extra money and start saving with your children for the thing you feel you can't afford. When you see your prayers answered, your children will know God is at hand to help your family.

3. Envisioning your future: As women, we put our needs last, often to the detriment of ourselves and our children. What is holding you back from your dreams for the future? What is the first step toward your dream life? Let me encourage you to take one small step—any step—toward your dream this month. Enroll in a class, write a page in your book, pull out a new canvas. Any small step will do. Plan now to take one more step next month.

My prayer for you, with my love

Dear God, we often feel under attack, even in our own families.

Please, for Your own Son's sake, bless my sister, so her children learn to trust You, too. If possible, allow her to avoid divorce by redeeming her marriage, since You are the Redeemer. Let her turn from harshness when dealing with the father of her children. If divorce is unavoidable, comfort her heart. Please bless her with the money and physical things she needs to provide for her children. Give her family deep understanding of how to comfort each other for the rest of their lives. Let laughter and joy ring out in her home.

Together, we claim Psalm 23:5–6 for her and her children, "You prepare a table before me in the presence of my enemies; You anoint my head with oil; My cup runs over. Surely goodness and mercy shall follow me All the days of my life; And I will dwell in the house of the LORD forever."

To pray for yourself

Good Father, You are the God who forgives. Help me remember what I saw in the father of my children, for their sakes. Help me forgive myself for the missteps I took along the path to this place. Give me the grace I need to keep forgiving the husband I once trusted. Help me see past my pain to the hero he wants to be in the lives of our children. Teach me to see beyond him and to trust You. You are unfailing in Your love for me. I praise You. Give me courage and patience today to keep focusing on the eternal, especially the best interests of my children. Teach me to love myself, reflecting the way You value and love me. Bless me now because that's Your heart's desire. In Jesus' name I pray. Amen.

"One reason people are unhappy today is because once they realize their cup is overflowing, they get a bigger cup." —**Pastor Anthony Williams**, Galilee Baptist Church, Tyler, Texas

CHAPTER NINETEEN

The Muscular Orderly

**How could paying attention
to spiritual reality change our marriages?**
By alerting us to our powerful allies.

ad loved being a surgeon, but being a patient was a whole different dynamic. When Dad woke up from open heart surgery years ago, he was convinced the ship was sinking and we needed to escape through the port hole. It took days for his brain to shake the anesthesia and come back to its normal coherent state. When he woke up from gall bladder surgery, he tried to talk David into calling a taxi so he could leave "this lovely resort with the great view."

One of my favorite post-anesthesia moments with Dad was when in a groggy medicated daze, he tried to comfort visitors in his hospital room with these words, "We won't worry about the subatomic structure of nuclear particles." Family members glanced in surprise at each other, racking our imaginations for what in the world he wanted us to know. "We won't sweat the small stuff!" shouted the first person to recognize one of Dad's favorite mottos.

When he woke up after the Code 44 moment, he had a clear, if somewhat confused, vision of what had happened.

"Who was the big orderly who carried me across the street when I was having my heart attack? I need to thank him," he said.

"Dad, there was no orderly carrying you and no heart attack. You coded, and they took you to ICU on a gurney where you were in a medically induced coma for two weeks. Then, when you were ready for therapy, we pushed you across the street in a wheelchair," I explained patiently. Practicing medicine for over thirty years trained my dad to care about the medical details. I knew his mind was booting back up and searching for his brain's deleted files. I repeated the sequence of events accurately each time he reviewed the information he was missing.

"Whatever happened to the guy who carried me across the street?" he would ask.

"There was no guy, Dad. Remember, we talked about this and here's what happened while you were out." Mom and I reassured him, repeated the facts, and emphasized the medical lingo so his brain could draw the logical conclusions on its own.

"There was a guy. He was big and muscular. I suffered cardiac arrest. I collapsed. He carried me himself, across the street. He did not push me in a wheelchair. He was very comforting and kind. He told me I would be all right. I want to thank him," insisted my dad again and again.

Finally, when we had been over the story many times, Dad began to believe me when I reminded him of the logical sequence of events. Why would an orderly carry him? Why would they go across to therapy before ICU? It didn't make sense.

One day I was telling a close friend, a champion prayer warrior, about the confusion my dad was suffering. She blinked and looked at me quizzically.

"Cathy, you better quit telling your dad he's wrong. What if an angel carried him back when his heart stopped!"

I'm not one to rule out an angel. We all know in crisis situations miracles sometimes defy the most logical explanation. Dad never wavered from his clear description. I picture our angel in crisp white scrubs, a burly man with bronze skin and a tender smile. So, I circled back and did the only sensible thing.

"Dad, I think I owe you an apology. I haven't been listening when you described your orderly. Now I think you were right. I bet you met an angel."

An angel was an explanation that satisfied us all.

Spiritual Instincts

In life, we tend to miss what should be obvious. We focus on the realty of the physical until our hearts disregard our spiritual instincts. Because I know God desires to have oneness with us forever, I easily believe for an instant my dad was suspended between this realm and the next. If so, it's no surprise he could clearly remember his experiences and the person he described in detail. There's something so comforting in the thought that an angel, or even perhaps Jesus, came to carry my dad in a spiritual realm. All the while we were praying and begging God for mercy as a family in crisis.

There are times in our lives when we need a miracle. The miracle we are seeking is a life marked by abiding fellowship. We don't always see miracles as they happen, though. Often, normal days fill up with the kind of challenges we all face on this earth. Sometimes, challenges evolve into a serious threat, even a crisis. Occasionally, we may even recognize our most significant relationships are suddenly spinning out of control.

For instance, someone we love may be whisked away to ICU. Or perhaps our marriages need life support. In an instant, life changes. In those moments, I know from firsthand experience there's an army of willing support surrounding us, if we are only alert to all the possibilities. I hope you don't ever experience a coma to become aware of the kind of support available to you in a heavenly realm.

Angels Unaware

Most of us experience another kind of spiritual help introduced to us through a Savior who entered our earthly realm in humility and unselfish service. Spiritual friends can provide the support and comfort we need. Our neighbor Shirley always calls our son her angel unaware (see Hebrews 13:2) because he made a point of pushing her garbage can to the street when he was growing up. It's not exactly the traditional interpretation, but Shirley's forte is applying what the Bible says in unexpected and inspiring ways.

One of the silver linings of struggling to hold our marriage together was when I began to recognize a host of women friends who became my angels unaware. God had prepared me for the moment when things began to unravel by surrounding me with strong godly warrior women friends. Much like my dad's muscled orderly, we all need good women who tenderly comfort our breaking hearts. Such friends carry us through tough days with wisdom, humor, and lots and lots of prayer.

Now, when I consider the benefits of those friendships, I wouldn't change a minute of the struggles David and I faced. We needed to sort out how we could live together harmoniously. I was tired of co-existing, tired of failed conversations and arguments. I wanted us to cherish each other again.

By living openly and telling the truth about the pain we were experiencing, I gained the comfort and friendship of some amazing women. I chose authenticity and in the process gained a life lived alongside fellow warrior women. Plus, they kept me sane when folks offered terrible advice along the way.

The Comfort of a Strong Helper

One example prominently comes to mind when it comes to the way God uses women. Have you ever heard folks scold women for trying to be "their husbands' Holy Spirit"? I get their gist. As women we should not underestimate our husband's ability to recognize the spiritual realm or to listen for God's voice. However, those same teachers do us a disservice when they fail to point out an important truth. Jesus links God's nature of comforting and helping with the wife's role.

Our loving help in our husbands' lives includes a commitment to the truth. Jesus comforts the disciples, telling them He will ask God to send another Helper, His Holy Spirit. If we are alert, we catch onto a life-changing idea. The Holy Spirit empowers us to help our husband.

We can assure the man we love he is a son of the good Father, not an orphan. It is so important for our husband, our sons, our brothers, even our dad, to know they have a good Father who is watching out for them in crisis. We, too, must keep in mind our special status as God's own beloved child.

"And I will pray the Father, and He will give you another Helper, that He may abide with you forever—the Spirit of truth, whom the world cannot receive, because it neither sees Him nor knows Him; but you know Him, for He dwells with you and will be in you. I will not leave you orphans; I will come to you" (John 14:16–18).

Wise Helpers

We can't help but notice that the concept is similar to the one in Genesis, "So Adam gave names to all cattle, to the birds of the air, and to every beast of the field. But for Adam there was not found a helper comparable to him" (Genesis 2:20). The Scriptures closely link our role of being alert for truth to our role as a strong helper. As women, we inherited our foremother Eve's desire to seek out wisdom. Is it any wonder the devil immediately saw opportunity in Eve's strongest asset, her desire to help her husband and provide comforting, strengthening wisdom?

"Then the serpent said to the woman, 'You will not surely die. For God knows that in the day you eat of it your eyes will be opened, and you will be like God, knowing good and evil.' So when the woman saw that the tree *was* good for food, that it *was* pleasant to the eyes, and a tree desirable to make *one* wise, she took of its fruit and ate. She also gave to her husband with her, and he ate" (Genesis 3:4–6).

In a spiritual realm where so much unseen happens all around us, wise women understand our resources and the temptations we face due to our perceptiveness. The enemy of our souls would like to tempt us to take on more responsibility than we should, discounting our trust in God. Satan would like to divide and conquer us in our marriage. He desires to destroy our unity. Our enemy would like for us to feel alone, abandoned, isolated, helpless, and afraid. He wants us to believe we are orphans. Heaven forbid! Not only do we want to be wise helpers to our husband and family, but we also want to seek out wisdom, too.

Wise Warrior Women

We are beloved children of a Father who surrounds us with a host of good women. We are witnesses to each other's lives and marriages. Like God's own beautiful Holy Spirit, our friends can be our strong helpers, too. They are waiting to offer a word of encouragement if we only claim the beautiful friendships God prepares for us as a blessing. Like our mother Eve, women are natural wisdom seekers.

Additionally, in a spiritual realm we cannot see, angels wait with strong arms to carry us when we faint. Jesus Himself will surround us with allies and mount an army to our defense.

His Holy Spirit is our Commander-in-Chief, the One who lovingly demonstrates how to wield truth like a double-edged sword, cutting between what is false and our responsive hearts. "For the word of God *is* living and powerful, and sharper than any two-edged sword, piercing even to the division of soul and spirit, and of joints and marrow, and is a discerner of the thoughts and intents of the heart" (Hebrews 4:12).

As crazy as it sounds to talk about angels, it's even crazier to think we are alone when it comes to our marriage or any of our relationships. God gave you a nature designed for a special role in your husband's life. You have the full power at your disposal of being a natural wisdom seeker, but you must be alert to an enemy who would like to thwart your glorious success. If that role seems overwhelming at times, no worries, we are not alone.

With such a good and powerful Father, we are certainly not orphans. Instead each one of us belongs in a sisterhood of women who have each other. As if that's not enough, we have the full resources of an angelic army working quietly behind the scenes to accomplish the good plan God has for each of us. Because God loves us wholeheartedly. Thoroughly. Unfailingly.

Marriage's ultimate purpose demonstrates oneness to a world with no other hope but companionship with God. Clearly, God will not abandon you. Like my dad, I am convinced there's an angel standing ready to carry you when no one else is looking.

In Case You Were Wondering...

Where do I find friends? We all crave fellowship with like-hearted people who welcome us. Are there people at church or in a nonprofit who share your passions? This is the common advice people give about where to find friends and it has merit. But there's more to the story.

True fellowship is a rare treasure in this world, even among like-minded people who share interests. Since we only keep what we give away, you may have to create a fellowship-rich environment for others. Few people know how to initiate loving relationships, so the responsibility may fall on you.

When we feel discouraged, knowing we are not alone comforts our souls. However, when searching for trustworthy friends, one big obstacle seems to be a recurring theme among successful women: comparing and competing.

Comparing and competing can be a symptom of self-righteousness. Freedom from self-righteousness comes at a deep level of embracing our worthiness before a God of unfailing love. That sounds sort of idealistic, but practice makes perfect. Oops, I meant to say practicing admitting our imperfection makes us free indeed. I know. Whoever heard of practicing to be less perfect? Yet, we all have more allies to see us through troubles when we let down our guard.

I especially hope you know what a valuable gift your friendship is. I hope you give fellowship generously and freely to all you meet. If you do, loving companionship will come back to you.

Pause, Ponder, Pray, and then Proceed

Nothing beats a strong ally when we are fighting a battle to strengthen fellowship in our marriages. Possibly, an army of strong allies may be what the doctor ordered! Let's go to God for help in our spiritual battles.

1. Understanding your needs: In what three specific areas of your life could you use an ally today? Which women stand out as a spiritual gift especially for you from God? Make a list of three strong friends. Now call or write them to say how much they mean to you.

2. Identifying your worth: What encounters felt like divine appointments for you this week? If possible, follow up with a new friend to offer her an encouraging word. Reaching out doesn't have to be hard. Just texting a favorite verse or saving her a seat at the next meeting will do. What do your friends say about you when they thank you? Make a list of attributes your friends like about you. Send a friend the top ten attributes you love most about her.

3. Envisioning your future: When you think about your marriage, what specific ways is God using you to gently convey truth? Naturally, Jesus specialized in conveying truth in creative ways. Why not begin your own list of creative ways to convey truth? How does He use you to pray? Give the gift of anonymous prayer to someone you love right now in the quiet of your heart. God is listening.

My prayer for you, with my love

Dear God, the One who commands an army of angels in the heavenly realms, look upon this dear sister with favor. It's so easy to feel downtrodden, uncreative, and discouraged when we are busy wives and mothers. Give her strong trustworthy women to be her companions on this earth. Surround her with prayer champions who will fight on their knees on behalf of her marriage and family. Please make her aware of the strength You offer her through her allies. Alert her to possible angelic sightings. May her alliance with You be her greatest strength and joy.

Together, we acknowledge You, her true Champion, and pray for her heart, declaring, "Who is this King of glory? The LORD of hosts, He *is* the King of glory" (PSALM 24:10).

To pray for yourself:

Good Father, I present myself to You as a woman who sometimes feels alone, afraid, and abandoned. When I feel downtrodden, Lord, uplift me. Draw me into Your arms and carry me to an inner place of safety and peace. When I feel discouraged, let me claim the justification offered by Your Son. Open my eyes to the allies You have given me in heavenly realms and here on Earth. Help me open my heart to the people You bring into my life today. Teach me to press past my fear and live victoriously today. Thank You for surrounding me with good women. Allow me to strengthen others. Strengthen my husband to be a spiritual warrior. Bless me now because that's Your heart's desire. In Jesus' name I pray. Amen.

"Therefore we also, since we are surrounded by so great a cloud of witnesses, let us lay aside every weight, and the sin which so easily ensnares us, and let us run with endurance the race that is set before us, looking unto Jesus, the author and finisher of our *faith, who for the joy that was set before Him endured the cross, despising the shame, and has sat down at the right hand of the throne of God."*—**Hebrews 12:1–2**

CHAPTER TWENTY

Best Moment in History to be Married

How is now the best moment in all history to be married?

We are free us to choose gratitude for the sisterhood of women who came before us.

David drove a gold 1976 T-top Corvette when I met him, circling the parking lot at the local lakeside hang out like the king of all things water-related. When I tell the story to small children, David is a dashing knight in shining armor mounted on a golden steed. Sometimes he is a cowboy riding in on a palomino. Yep, horses seem to be a recurring theme. In fact, my grown children still giggle when I throw in the part about his golden hair streaming behind him in the wind. What can I say? It was the '70s, and men needed haircuts.

The story is so much funnier because David does not remember the first time we met. I think his memory fail reflects how astute he was. I was still in high school and too young to date him anyway. Besides, his memory lapse allows me to tell the story with as much melodramatic flair as I can include with a clear conscience.

Little did we know, when he discovered me for real, how quickly thirty years would pass. Like a blink. Sitting on the pier with that first picnic basket and nothing but dreams, we talked about all the big questions.

You know the tricky stuff, like would we have our kids sprinkled or wait for immersion baptism. My first clue he is a better negotiator than me surfaced around the issue of dancing. He wasn't much of a dancer, and I was pretty sure God intended for me to go through life dancing at every opportunity. David convinced me it was God's will for us to marry in spite of the fact our height difference virtually proved otherwise.

We were so naive, holding hands and sharing our first breathless kiss. Occasionally, I wonder if the deck was stacked against us, even way back then. Was it easier to be married happily before no-fault divorce made going separate ways a tempting option? What about the days when societal pressure enforced long-term commitment? Did the old days provide better incentives to work together at being happy?

Imagine my surprise when, while researching for this book, I discovered now is actually the best time in history to be married. I find that encouraging somehow. I hope you do, too.

Now is the best moment in history to be married? You've got to be kidding, Cathy! How could that possibly be true? Oh, but it is true. Why? Because never before have women enjoyed so many options and so much of their own decision-making freedom.

Why focus on the women who came before us? Because our mothers and grandmothers created durable marriages—even happy ones sometimes—with a whole lot less freedom than we enjoy today. So, I celebrate the sisterhood of women who came before us.

Marriage's Surprising History

By understanding what women before us faced, we can gratefully live large in our moment of history. Generations of women before us would trade places with us in a heartbeat if they could live now, defining their own lives and marriages. We are indeed a blessed generation of women!

A quick recap of the history of marriage empowers our grateful hearts to rejoice, making us very sexy modern women. Yep, joy and gratitude characterize sexy, confident women, and better yet, joy and gratitude do not require a diet, workout clothes, or a gym membership. Glory!

I would be remiss if I didn't mention that, while the suffrage movement started in the mid-1800s, women only gained the right to vote both in Britain and the U.S. in the early 1900s.

Perhaps even more surprising, this moment in history constitutes the best era ever for married men. For instance, into the early 1900s, men were expected to marry for politically or economically expedient reasons. Because their extended family orchestrated a man's marriage, the culture-at-large winked when men pursued intimacy in whatever pathetic leftover ways they could find. Try to imagine anything as wounding as a man forced into a marriage that did not meet his own needs.

Or imagine being female and young in the 1920s and thrown in the "newly expanded 'juvenile court system'" because promiscuity was labeled "delinquent" behavior, and therefore, illegal.[39]

Men had it just as bad due to eugenics. Eugenics means if your genetic makeup tops the socially acceptable charts, you get to reproduce lots of kids. If not, society could sterilize you without your consent, often without your knowledge at all. A decade or two before the Nazis rose to power in Germany, California had the "most extensive eugenics program in the world."[40] "Most of the men were sterilized because they were unable to perform the breadwinner role, in other words because they didn't have a job. Three-fourths of the sterilized women were 'sex delinquents.'"[41]

Throughout history, courageous women found ways to claim independence, in spite of pressure to conform. Knowing the risk gives us a whole new respect for women like Mae West, who was ahead of her time in the 1920s in her outspokenness. "I'm single because I was born that way," she said.[42]

Reinventing the family farm

Throughout history most couples worked together on the farm or,

---

39 Stephanie Coontz, *Marriage, a History: How Love Conquered Marriage* (New York: Penguin Books, 2005), 212.

40 Ibid.

41 Ibid.

42 Mae West Quotes, https://www.goodreads.com/author/quotes/259666.Mae_West, accessed 09-21-16

as the industrial age developed, in small retail businesses where the whole family produced much of what they sold.

During WWII, women joined the home-front effort, often taking jobs vacated by servicemen. Afterwards, however, media blitzes extolled the virtues of women who stayed home with the children. Women who tried to hold onto their jobs as the men returned home were branded unpatriotic.[43]

If you tend toward the entrepreneurial and you are dreaming of spending invigorating days working side by side with your husband, you now have more opportunity than ever before, especially with all the unlimited internet possibilities. At our house, we call working together in a family business reinventing the family farm.

Many people may view the 1950s as the perfect time to be married in some ways, but all was not well. "As early as 1957 divorce rates started rising again in the United States and several other countries. In fact, one of every three American couples who married in the 1950s eventually divorced."[44]

However, it was not until 1975 when it finally "became illegal to require a married woman to have her husband's written permission to get a loan or a credit card."[45] To give you an idea of how recent that was, I applied for my first credit card in college only a few years after the law changed, without needing the approval of anyone else. Who knew!

More Time Than Ever to Be Married

One last thing I find encouraging in a weird way. Up until modern times, life expectancies were short, in part due to child-birth mortality and the lack of penicillin. Penicillin was only available for widespread use at the end of WWII in the late 1940s.[46] For a variety of reasons,

43 Stephanie Coontz, *Marriage, a History,* 231–233
44 Ibid., 252
45 Ibid., 255.
46 Katie Kalvaitis, "Penicillin: An accidental discovery changed the course of medicine," https://www.healio.com/news/endocrinology/20120325/penicillin-an-accidental-discovery-changed-the-course-of-medicine, accessed 02-08-17.

including better health care, life expectancies changed radically. Both men and women saw a life expectancy increase greater than twenty years between 1920 and 2000.[47]

When we think of marriages lasting fifty to sixty years, we are witnessing a miracle. By working to create a great lasting marriage in this modern age of longer lives, our accomplishment is unique in history. We are among the first generations who have the opportunity to live for such a long time together in marriage. Maybe that's why it's so dang hard! Yet, we have more time than ever to create the beautiful marriage we want.

We hear much gloom and doom when it comes to marriage. I just couldn't finish this book without including some positive historical conclusions. Today, more than any other time in history, men and women have the power to make the decisions most authentic to their hearts. We get to decide with whom we will spend our lives. Plus, we live longer to boot!

If we realize we have made a terrible mistake, we have the best options ever available, including counseling. Even the drastic decision to divorce includes more equitable laws now. Fortunately, with education and jobs available to hard-working people of both genders, no one stays married because of social traps.

In the United States and many parts of the world, it's still safe to worship as a family on Sunday morning if we choose to. No one busts down our doors if we skip church. We can freely pray for those parts of the world where religious liberty is not tolerated.

We buy, sell, or rent homes, apartments, and condos best suited for our families with no restrictions except what we can afford. We freely pursue education. Or start a business. Or do both simultaneously.

Additionally, we enjoy the best options ever available when it comes to birth control and fertility. We expect our children to experience the same freedom. Because of life expectancies, we have more time than anyone else throughout history to develop a fellowship-based mar-

---

47 "1900–2000: Changes in Life Expectancy in the United States," https://www.elderweb.com/book/appendix/1900-2000-changes-life-expectancy-united-states, accessed 02-08-17.

riage. Additionally, God willing, we can assume we'll get to spend time with the next generation, too, given improved life expectancies.

The Society of Amazing Women

Thank you for reading all the way to this point. We loved sharing our family stories. Before we close these marriage conversations, I want to acknowledge the many amazing women who grieve because their moms weren't there for them. It is hard to figure out how to have healthy marriage conversations without the guiding presence of a good mom.

Perhaps your mother passed away while you were too young to go without mothering. Some of my dearest friends experienced the heartbreak of a mom who was emotionally wounded. If a traumatic experience is part of your history, please take heart.

When we think about our own spot in the sisterhood of amazing women throughout history, our moms always seem to find a way into our stories, for better or worse. If you are like most women, you think your mom is awesome even as she makes you a little crazy simultaneously. What is it about moms?

If your mom is still with you, please, be kind to her now because eventually she will be gone. You won't harbor regrets for being a kind daughter.

If your mom has issues, boundaries may be required. All moms have baggage. Plus, some moms have mental health issues. Please consult a professional if you suspect more to the story with your mom. Feel free to structure the time you spend with her, limiting visits to things you can handle.

We must make decisions to serve the whole family's best interests. Your husband can probably offer a perspective about your mother's mental health. If he helps you find appropriate boundaries, this may actually strengthen your marriage.

One thing that changed the dynamics of my relationship with my mom was when the Lord showed me I had to grow up and love her in the places where she still struggled.

Mom was a very orderly, methodical person, even in her most creative moments. I depended on her impeccable brain to remind me of a thousand small responsibilities I tend to overlook daily. I'm pretty sure my forgetfulness wore her out when I was a child.

She never really got my seemingly chaotic creativity until her health and memory faded as she aged. Suddenly I was her flexible friend with ideas for overcompensating about forgetfulness. It was a new era for us, one I prepared for by loving her in her frailties long before she realized she had them.

Nothing takes the place of the comfort a mom can offer. If your own mom has passed away, lives far away, or failed you, you are in luck anyway. It may sound a little heartless but getting to choose who you let mother you instantly frees you somehow.

Blessedly, countless widows, wondering if their lives have any purpose left, grace every community. By initiating a friendship with an older woman, you create one of those God moments where everyone gets a blessing. In my church, we address all the older women as Mother, a title before their names as a mark of respect. Honestly, we can't have too many godly mothers!

O Blessed Generation of Women

We all need to be mothered sometimes, no matter how long we live. Life dishes out sweet surprises we want to share. In the next moment we may find ourselves hanging in there, holding our marriage together by our unmanicured fingernails.

No matter what's happening in your life or marriage today, you can surround yourself with strong women. Plus, we can treasure the women in history who made this moment possible for us all.

Before my beautiful mom died, she generously shared her stories for this book. I miss her very much, especially as we go to press now. If you like, may I invite you to adopt her as a mother figure? Mom would have welcomed you with open arms! She would love to think of you and how you take inspiration from her fortitude and compassion.

At Camp Krafve we depend on a group of amazing women warriors we think of as the Fireside Tribe. They help us decide what our podcast and blog topics will be; they offer accountability and correction; they encourage us with wisdom. Often, our Fireside Tribe includes other women who are creating positive messages, too. We love supporting their efforts. You are invited to join together with us in the adventure of affecting change in our culture with positive messages. You can find us at our website, CathyKrafve.com.

No matter your personal experience, you are naturally part of our expansive sisterhood of awesome women throughout history who welcome you and me into their society. You get to be the kind of woman who leaves a legacy for those who follow.

In this good moment in history, we tend to take our blessings for granted. We owe gratitude to the mighty women who came before us. When you think about what they went through to get us here now, we owe it to them to be positively awesome. Out of respect for the sisterhood of women, we can build relationships with patience and joy. I offer my sincere prayer for your mighty success, in marriage and in life! Today is the best moment in history to be married. May you cherish your marriage with joy!

In Case You Were Wondering...

What if I am plagued by identity crisis or insecurity? We all are—there's no "what if" about it! But you can turn to God's Spirit for the best truth about who you are. You are a human with a spirit. He has chosen you for this moment in history for a reason.

We can conquer our insecurities and put them in their place with a little reality check. Haven't we all heard a weird noise at night when we are home alone? Did your fear make you open all the closet doors? In that same way, we need to separate the truth from our false assumptions, like a gal with a giant flashlight at home alone.

Fear and insecurity are not just noises in the night. They are powerful emotions, prompting us to be brave and courageous if we let them.

Plus, we can turn to the God of all comfort, who understands our fears and completely comprehends our true identity as His beloved children.

"For the eyes of the LORD run to and fro throughout the whole earth, to show Himself strong on behalf of *those* whose heart *is* loyal to Him" (2 Chronicles 16:9a).

Nothing encourages me like knowing God loves me with unfailing devotion. He intends for us to be successful at the plans He has for us. I want you to include yourself in the sisterhood of amazing women throughout history.

You are dear to God's heart. Rather than co-existing, I pray you will cherish those you love, starting with yourself and your husband. Together, may you have authentic marriage conversations too innumerable to count in the days ahead!

Pause, Ponder, Pray, and then Proceed

I hope you rejoice to be part of the best moment in history for marriage. Families all around us need shoring up, whether or not you are married. Thankfully, we are the most fortunate of women in a long tradition of amazing women. Oh, the blessings we enjoy!

1. Understanding your needs: With your own personal time machine, which moment of history would you like to check out and why? What women in history faced similar challenges to the ones you face? Give yourself the gift of more time to read this year. Include a historical biography on your list.

2. Identifying your worth: Make a note in your journal—why do you think a loving God chose now for your moment in history? If you knew your marriage decisions now would impact your family for generations after you are gone, what's the most important thing you would do today? Ask a friend to pray with you for you to be bold about fulfilling the plans God has for you.

3. Envisioning your future: What will your children say about the marriage you helped create? If you could communicate your way to one dream-come-true moment in your marriage next week or next month,

what would that moment look like? Please pray about prompting a healthy marriage conversation with your husband tonight. I am praying the word *cherish* will permeate all aspects of your marriage and life.

My prayer for you, with my love

Dear God, the One who set the earth on its axis rotating around the sun, we praise You for Your ongoing presence throughout history. We get distracted by any little tidbit on the nightly news, letting ranting and gossip take over our thoughts. We get critical and angry. We crave truth and settle for trends. Yet, we see Your mercy and grace extended to generations.

We praise You because You allow us to live in the best moment in history for marriage. I thank You for this sister, Your beautiful daughter. Her future and the future of her family are secure in You alone. Before the sun sets on another day deepen her sense of Your companionship. Let her know she is cherished by You!

Together, we claim this from Psalm 25 for her and for all the people she will influence in her lifetime, "Show me Your ways, O LORD; Teach me Your paths. Lead me in Your truth and teach me, For You *are* the God of my salvation; On You I wait all the day" (Psalm 25:4–5).

To pray for yourself

Lord Jesus, You intercede for me even when I am unaware. Help me focus my attention on You. When I feel angry, create healing in my heart so I can let go of old wounds. Allow me the privilege of influence. Give me insight and tenderness about the needs of those around me.

Gratefully, I acknowledge I live in the most exciting moment in history. Please help me to walk in freedom so You are glorified in my life. You are good, and I love You. I want to cherish You. I am Your grateful daughter, the one whom You bless. In Jesus' name I pray. Amen.

"My most brilliant achievement was my ability to be able to persuade my wife to marry me." —**Winston Churchill**

More Adventures to Come

What is *not* out there in the marketplace of ideas?
*Practical, biblically grounded truth seems
to be hard to find amid all the clatter.*

Omid roses and chocolate, he lavished a candlelit dinner on her. He wrote poetry to celebrate his love for her. He didn't want her to miss out. So, he celebrated what would have been her fiftieth wedding anniversary to her first husband as if it was their own.

A few days before the big event, he noticed she was sad. They would not live long enough to have their own fiftieth anniversary together. Divorced for years from her first husband, she shared this story with me in hushed whispers because she could hardly believe the tenderness of her second husband. How romantic is that!

In all, before she passed away, they celebrated over thirty anniversaries together—plus one fiftieth anniversary. Her husband's tender, creative response to her pain illustrates just how intimacy uniquely blossoms in each marriage.

If Cinderella and Barbie taught us anything, we know Hollywood is good at marketing movies and products, but bad at teaching us healthy beliefs about relationships. We all want happily ever after. Happy can be as simple as rebooting to a more functional definition of marriage. Marriage specifically develops uniquely for the two people who create it, like my friends who celebrated their unique version of a fiftieth anniversary.

We all want to retreat to our happy place, our home. We all face daily challenges at work, in our extended families, and in our public lives. At home, we don't want to get by just co-existing.

We want to relax, laugh, have inside jokes, and finish each other's sentences. Armed with a definition of marriage endorsed by the One who designed marriage, we can freely search out practical strategies, allowing us to cherish each other.

It won't hurt us to think about what makes us happy when it comes to marriage. In fact, knowing what we want will help us create the marriage conversations we crave. With so many marriages around us failing, I am glad you are thinking about how success in your home looks to you. This crucial information is supremely personal.

There's a tendency in our culture to want to exclude God from any talk in the public conversation. Sadly, when Christians do engage, we often sound dogmatic and argumentative. Missing the "God piece" impacts everything else, however. We must keep finding gentle ways to have tender conversations with people we love. Out of authentic, deeply spiritual conversations come the daily mini miracles.

The greatest miracle of all is that God loves me. He loves you. He loves us exactly as we are. In exactly this moment and these circumstances, whatever they are. He keeps loving us, even when we don't love ourselves. When we go so far as to reject Him, He keeps seeking us out. I hope some of my stories captured this truth, reminding your heart to embrace wholeness and delight.

I wanted a super-smart word for what you are, so I Googled synonyms. Perceptive, astute, insightful, intuitive. In an unrelated, but funny way, smart means high-fashioned. I think you are all those things. Even with our culture so confused and distressed on the controversial topic of marriage, you can negotiate for the marriage perfectly suited to you. I hope you are sighing with relief and happiness. Maybe you have some tough but constructive work ahead of you. Hopefully, as you read, you gained some fresh ideas about how to enhance your own marriage with great conversations.

God designed marriage to be such a creative process that no two marriages are alike. Victory starts with healthy marriage conversations. Small daily victories move us in the right direction. We have many resources for change. For instance, my personal collection of books on marriage was far cheaper than all the counseling we invested in. Collecting and reading books, plus counseling, sure beats the cost of divorce. You can listen to a podcast for free while you multitask on the treadmill.[48]

If you received anything from this book, I hope this simple truth sticks in your mind—the smallest change can be transformative. I hope your head spins from all the creative ideas you might like to try at your house this week. My prayer for you is you claim the courage God offers you and try something new.

I am so proud of you for reading to the end of this book. People tell me all the time they are not readers. Thank you for reading. It means so much to me. I hope you will go to CathyKrafve.com and share your thoughts and stories with me. You are the reason I write. Hearing from you is my great joy.

We live in the best time to be married. I respect your ability and your privilege to think for yourself. As you consider what makes you happy in marriage, please think as long as you like. Ask as many hard questions as you need to. I have already told you I think you are smart. You can identify what you want and figure out how to move in the direction of accomplishing your relationship goals.

After a long day at camp as a youngster, I used to fall asleep dreaming of tomorrow's adventures. I pray you wake up tomorrow with this phrase in your head, "More adventures to come."

---

48 We have a bunch of amazing podcasts picked out for you at https://CathyKrafve. com/fireside-talk-radio/, created by modern heroes of the faith. I hope you check them out and enjoy the hilarious, truthful, and insightful people who share all kinds of cool stuff just for you.

I am Grateful

First, I want to thank CrossRiver Media. Publisher Tamara Clymer understood this project from the first moment we met, sharing her sacred stories of growing up with parents who prayed together. Wise and patient editor Debra L. Butterfield held me accountable for every word and became a cherished friend in the process. Through author relations specialist Deedee Lake's big and beautiful heart, I discovered the strong warrior women connected with CrossRiver. They provided invaluable wisdom on how to market the project and take care of myself as I poured out my heart on these pages.

When Karen Neumair of Credo Literary Agency joined me in this adventure, I felt as though the dream could be real. Thank you, Karen, for all the years you honed your craft, creating relationships throughout the industry, while I daydreamed of a future where other readers like myself would take a few hours to read something I wrote.

I am grateful to God for the talented, media savvy, and wise Sandra Beck of Beck Multi-media. Sandra, just as your innumerable media talents and skills bless me, your amazing heart touches and influences my life daily. Thank you for believing in this project when I was afraid to.

Sandra further blessed me by introducing me to a squad of Dynamic Women,[49] who epitomize the ideas expressed in this book with their

---

49 For more amazing podcasts from Dynamic Women, go to DynamicWomenTalkRadio,com.

willingness to talk respectfully and freely about any topic. Specifically, I want to thank Robyn Boyd, Linda Kreter, and Frankie Picasso.

Christi McGuire stayed with me word for word back when the manuscript was a messy pile of random ideas. What an astonishing example you are of a mighty modern woman with a huge heart and so much skill!

I also benefited from the talent, expertise, and beautiful hearts of the people I turn to with my tech questions: Margie Boyd, Roy Bryan, Ben Chapman, Yazirri "YO" Orrostieta, and Dan Velie.

Thank you to Martha Hook who, along with giving me pep talks, encouraged me to attend the Mt. Hermon Christian Writer's Conference. There I met Inger Logelin, who took me under her wing, befriending me at a crucial moment when my mother died. Who, but God, could explain the coincidence that you share Mom's birthday, Inger?

I am thankful for those Bible scholars, writers, and pastors whose encouragement and correction fuel my confidence. They include Bobby Dagnel, James Dill, David Dykes, Chris Legg, Ben A. Simpson, Ross Strader, Byron Henderson, and my own head pastor at Galilee Baptist Church, Anthony Williams.

As with so many other communicators in our generation, Paul and Cathy Powell gave me courage at a strategic moment to keep writing what I believe to be true. Along with those dear friends, I count on a trusted group of women to pray bravely, pounding the throne room with integrity, humility, and confidence. Thank You, O Lord, for hearing our prayers.

A special thanks goes to people who passed along wisdom and listened patiently to my insecurities: Joyce Lynn Arrington, Charla Autrey, Bruce Brookshire, Paula Brookshire, Gina Butler, Shirley Callon, Jenny Clark, Grace and John English, Charles Fries, Kathryn Gohmert, Ann Howard, Leslie Jones, Les Krafve, Will Krafve, Randy and Diane McGirr, Charlie Niven, Brad and Diane Onstadt, Anna Pierce, Emily Primer, Judy Robinette, Doris Sharpe, and Ellen Trant. Hopefully, your influence and compassion show in my life.

For invaluable help with the manuscript early on: Susan Andreone, Kristi Boyette, Bobbie Dance, Janine Islam, Fritter McNally, Travis

Trant, and Aubrey Sharpe. Thanks to Pegi Eckert for trying to read the other never-to-be-seen-in-public books I tried to write along the way.

Without our Camp Krafve Fireside Tribe of amazing women, there would be no wise interactions, no thoughtful questioning, no one to hold me accountable and make me stretch deeper to that place in my soul where I long to give you the best. You inspire me. I thank God for you.

I am thankful for my children, grandchildren, and for the in-laws and amazing friends they bring into our lives.

Most of all, I am grateful for my beloved husband, David, who knows how to hang in there and love unconditionally, sharing the sacred with courage.

To God be all glory!

About the Author

Queen of Fun and Coffee Cup Philosopher, Cathy Krafve delivers creativity and encouragement on every page.

Host of Fireside Talk Radio, her weekly blogs and podcasts reach over two million listeners and readers annually. She understands companionship begins with authentic conversation.

With journalistic fervor and a knack for laughter and story-telling, Cathy puts a snappy spin on deeply spiritual truths. Her audiences learn to leverage compassion and courage in order to engage in two-way conversational adventures.

Join the Fireside Tribe as we create life so beautiful in its imperfection generations after us will be retelling our stories with joy and laughter.

Truth with a Texas twang spoken here!

Cathy loves it when reading and listening friends get in touch. Camp Krafve is about sharing real stuff she learned, probably the hard way. Please look for fun, free tools at CathyKrafve.com to help you create tender conversations. Or look for conversation-starting podcasts with experts on Fireside Talk Radio.

Hands Full
Thirty days of encouragement for busy moms
Available in bookstores and from online retailers.
CrossRiver Media
www.crossrivermedia.com

Discover more great books at CrossRiverMedia.com

AN UNNATURAL BEAUTY

Holiness is not an endless list of "thou shalt nots." It's not how we behave, what we think, or how we react or respond to life and the people around us. You'll discover foundational truths from Scripture, the path to a deeper, more intimate relationship with God, and why holiness can't be achieved through our own efforts. With relatable stories, Esther reminds us that Holiness is not a what, but a glorious Who, and He's inviting you to share in His divine nature.

M. ESTHER LOVEJOY

UNSHAKABLE FAITH

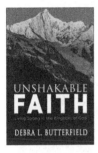

With *Unshakable Faith*, you'll build an indestructible foundation to your faith and crush your doubts. This 7-week Bible study contains 5 to 6 lessons per week, each lesson designed to be completed in 20 minutes or less. Topics covered include your kingdom identity, faith fundamentals, your authority and power, and your weapons and armor. You'll grow and strengthen your faith, learn faith fundamentals, and learn to command the power and authority God has given you.

UNBEATEN

Difficult times often leave Christians searching the Bible for answers to the most difficult questions—Does God hear me when I pray? Why isn't He doing anything? Author Lindsey Bell understands the struggle. As she searched the Bible for answers to these tough questions, her studies led her through the stories of biblical figures, big and small. She discovered that while life brings trials, faith brings victory. And when we rely on God for the strength to get us through, we can emerge *Unbeaten*.

THE GRACE IMPACT

The promise of grace pulses throughout Scripture. Chapter after chapter, the Bible shows a loving heavenly Father lavishing his grace on us through His son. In her book, *The Grace Impact*, author Nancy Kay Grace gives us a closer glimpse at God's character. His grace covers every detail of life, not just the good things, but the difficult, sad and complicated things. That knowledge can give us the ability to walk confidently through life knowing God is with us every step of the way.

the

Benefit

Package

30 days of
God's goodness
from Psalm 103

If you enjoyed this book, will you consider sharing it with others?

- Please mention the book on Facebook, Twitter, Pinterest, or your blog.

- Recommend this book to your small group, book club, and workplace.

- Head over to Facebook.com/CrossRiverMedia, 'Like' the page and post a comment as to what you enjoyed the most.

- Pick up a copy for someone you know who would be challenged or encouraged by this message.

- Write a review on Amazon.com, BN.com, or Goodreads.com.

- To learn about our latest releases subscribe to our newsletter at www.CrossRiverMedia.com.

Made in the USA
Monee, IL
03 June 2021